New DOST Intercultural Series
1

Editors: *Sisir Basu, Alessandro Monti, Carole Rozzonelli*

2015

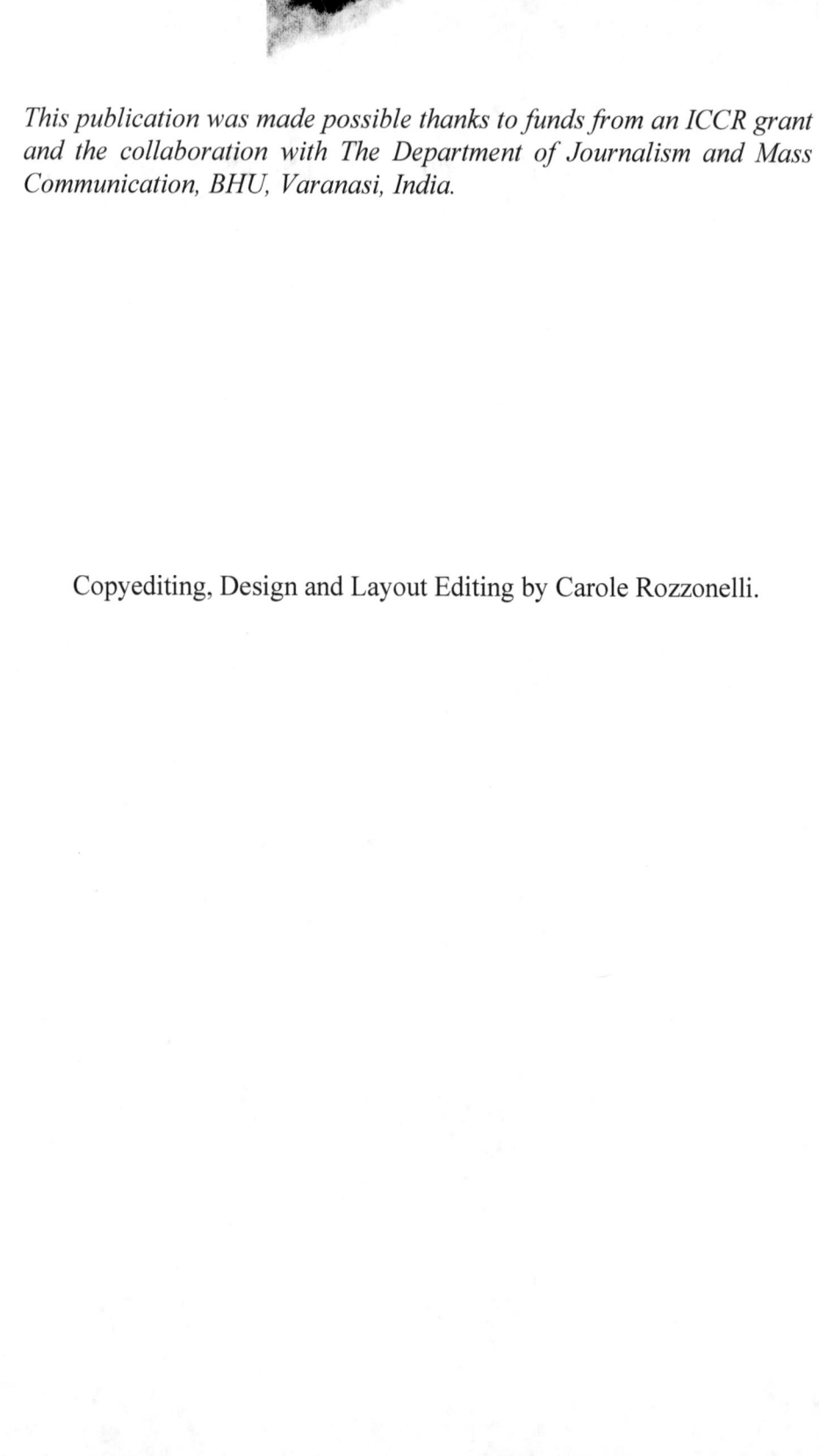

This publication was made possible thanks to funds from an ICCR grant and the collaboration with The Department of Journalism and Mass Communication, BHU, Varanasi, India.

Copyediting, Design and Layout Editing by Carole Rozzonelli.

Experiments in Film Appreciation

Editors:
Sisir Basu
Alessandro Monti
Carole Rozzonelli

NEW DOST EDITION
Italy - France

First published 2015 in the USA

Revised Edition, 2016

Print-on-demand Books and EBooks

Paperback ISBN: 978-1-326-41841-0

EBook ISBN: 978-1-326-34511-2

Published by NEW DOST EDITION

NEW DOST France, Lyon.
NEW DOST Italy, Torino.

Copyright © 2012 by THE NEW DOST PRESS

E-mail: alessandromonti_prof@yahoo.com

Acknowledgements:
Reproduction of material from *The Times of India*, *The Telegraph*,
The Hindu, and *The Indian Express* © 2011 All rights reserved.

Photo Credits: PTI (Cover Illustration), © Courtesy of PTI.

Cover Design by Carole Rozzonelli.

Book NEW DOST

Contents

Acknowledgements

This collection of articles concerning film appreciation is the fruitful result of an ICCR Fellowship (mid-January – mid-May 2011) with the Department of Journalism and Mass Communication at Banaras Hindu University. I came to share with the Head, Professor Sisir Basu, the scope and perspectives of my research, along with a handful of enthusiastic and well-schooled research students.

This volume (hopefully the first of a series) has been partially funded by my ICCR grant and constitutes an intercultural project, this time on Indian cinema, involving people in collaboration with several academic institutions, the University of Turin (Department of Oriental Studies), the University Lyon 2 (Institut de la Communication) and the Department of Journalism and Mass Communication at BHU.

A different version of *Experiments in Film Appreciation* has been simultaneously published in India.

Alessandro Monti

Editorial Note

Square Brackets [] in the text indicate editorial care.

A Brief Note. The Jersey of the Goddess: Sporting Ways to Nationhood.

Alessandro Monti

The image of the Goddess in the cover suggests a few considerations, concerning her particular iconography, in terms both of her belligerent aspect and of her association with the event of the World Cup of cricket in post-colonial India.[1] Sport and Hindu nationalism constitute the two facets of her numinous representation; for the violent side Professor Sisir Basu is dealing in this volume with the problem, whereas the association with sport and national identity will be broached here, with reference to cinematic imagination.

The nexus has been made explicit in *Lagaan (Tax on Land*, 2001), a period film which deals with the fictionalised birth of cricket in India, when a village plays a victorious game against an English team. The implied plea behind the story is meant to highlight unity and shared belonging through a multiplicity of identities, all of them enclosed and endorsed within a village. So the team cuts across casteism, religion and regionalism, since it includes, together with a Hindu majority, an untouchable, a Muslim and a Punjabi Sikh. It also comes somehow to terms with Hindu fundamentalism, through the half-grotesque figure of the village holy man.

Lagaan also introduces the theme of self-regulation (*swadeshi*), given how the village authorises itself against the English. In fact, the local raja allows the match, without giving however any help to the Indian team, whose operational autonomy is further stressed in the film by the deleting of a scene in which the sympathetic English young

---

[1] *The Telegraph*, Calcutta, 2 April 2011. Photo Credits: © 2011 Courtesy of The Press Trust of India Ltd.

woman supports it by giving the necessary equipment.[2] As a result the village stands for the uncompromised core of India, a feature which is also enforced by the unyielding attitude shown by the village hero in front of a possible love-story with the memsahib.

The centrality of the village in an imagined map of India has been made seminal since *Mother India* (1957), in which community ethos stands high against the individual rebellious attitude of the son. However, the starting sequence in *Mother India* of a caterpillar digging at a canal for irrigation, one suggesting a technological process supposed to change a timeless rural society, is crucially amplified in *Lagaan*, if one considers how much cricket means nowadays in India, in terms of modernity, post-colonial globalisation and above all of glamorous national business implying crores of money and a Bollywood hall of fame, since many teams are owned by famous actors (like Shah Ruck Khan), either men or women.

Thus the statue of the Goddess wearing the national jersey intimates not just an act of mimic extravaganza, but declares a Hindutva-like statement of militant and substantially excluding identity. The Hindu *trishul* and the hockey club are sponsored by the Goddess – they are meant both of them as weapons in an implied clash of cultures. Hindu identity and cricket represent jointly Indian nationhood in an assertive frame of general competition.

This discourse of corporate identity against and through the fragmentation of regionalism is central in the film *Chak De! India* (*Go! India*, 2007). Here a sport now marginal as hockey becomes the agency through which national unity and the transition to modernity are finally achieved. A Muslim player considered to be the responsible of a defeat against the Pakistani team is marginalised as a traitor to his motherland.[3] He succeeds in taking charge of the women's national team of hockey,

---

[2] It should be observed how in *Swadesh, We the People* (2004) the modernisation of a timeless village needs the intervention of an expatriate scientist, one who contrives "country-made" electricity for the Backwards.

[3] In real life this episode has its counterpart in the controversial marriage of the Indian tennis player Sania Mirza with the Muslim cricket champion from Pakistan. As a reaction, a petrol pump in the supposedly modernised Bangalore has "cut out the tennis star's face off hoardings, following her marriage to Pakistani cricketer Shoaib Malik". The reason why has been given as follows, "Customers would drive into the petrol pump and ask us why we have posters of the girl who married a Pakistani. So we decided to remove her face." (*Hindustan Times*, New Delhi, 18 April 2010).

against the supposed better opinion of the responsible board, which would not allow participation in the world competition.

However, the trainer leads the team to victory, notwithstanding they initially stand as an ill-assorted medley of uncooperative and quarrelling individuals. Its heteroclite composition reflects on the wrong side Indian difference in nationhood, since it includes semi-tribals from the North, Buddhists from Himachal Pradesh, a Punjabi Sikh, Tamils, Keralites, a Christian Anglo-Indian (from a Railway colony), etc. Apparently the cohesive unity shown previously on the screen by the traditional village yields here to regional fragmentation – as a matter of fact the *chalta hai* (thus goes the world) attitude flaunted at first by the team is brought to discipline – even if cooperation on the field between the two star players is just achieved as a hat trick in the final match.

The attained sense of nationhood is progressively endorsed in the film by means of the Raisina Hill and Lodi Park locations throughout the first part of *Chak De! India*, whereas the turning point in the collective consciousness of the team shifts the emblematic site to a modern and westernising eating place, in which eve-teasing is answered by the girls with an explosion of corporate feminine counterviolence. Their joint reaction against intimated passivity echoes back in terms of gender the rebellion of the peasants in *Lagaan* – it instructs the full passage of the girls into modernity and that is exactly this numinous step that authorises as it were the wished for sponsoring, concerning jerseys and clubs, etc., on behalf of the so far neglected and despised team.

Both the Goddess in our cover figure and the women players are given the national jersey, as a token of legitimising authority; in particular the latter are authorised to represent the nation. Their dispersal across the country makes nationalist *tirthas* (or sites of passage) of their places of origin, which are now inscribed *de iure* into the metaphorical and metaphysical map of India.

Films cited

Mother India, Mehboob Khan, 1957.

Lagaan, Ashutosh Gowariker, 2001.

Swadesh, We the People, Ashutosh Gowariker, 2004.

Chak De! India, Shimit Amin, 2007.

The Tragedy of Gujarat 2002 Haunts: A Look at Three Films[1] that Made the Tragedy as the Backdrop.

Sisir Basu

Let me begin this article with a personal note. I was stationed in the northeast India when the tragedy of Gujarat in the year 2002 took place. My only connection with the rest of the country and the world was then a radio. I was an ardent listener of the BBC World Service. The national newspaper would reach me a day late and most of the time later than that.

My landlord was a devout Hindu and would perform his longish daily rituals at least twice a day. He, in my opinion, was a simple and humble man. His courtesy and decency were imprinted in his behavior. I was keeping track of what was happening in Gujarat after the Godhra incident and the riot/massacre of the people that followed. From the news reports, I could gather that something unusual was happening in Gujarat. This was not the usual riot (so called) that generally takes place in the communally sensitive spots dotting India.

After listening to the radio news bulletin, one evening, as I was going out of the residence for some work, I met my landlord who had just finished his rituals and was standing near the gate. We greeted each other as usual. I told him then about what was happening in Gujarat such as I had heard in the radio news bulletin. I told him that the Muslims were being butchered. The reply was that they (Muslims) deserved this, they should be taught a lesson. I made my way out as I could not proceed with any kind of exchange or dialogue with him. I

---

[1] The three films are *Parzania* directed by Rahul Dholakia (2007), *Firaaq* directed by Nandita Das (2009), and *Mr. and Mrs. Iyer* (2002) directed by Aparna Sen. [This article was written before the ascent of Modi to national power].

have been haunted with his mindset ever since. What is it that divides the people so completely?

Siddharth Varadarajan starts his book *Gujarat: the Making of a Tragedy* with this paragraph: "On 27ᵗʰ February, at approximately ten minutes to eight in the morning, the Sabarmati Express fitfully pulled out of Godhra railway station on the last leg of what was to be one of the most catastrophic rail journeys of post-partition India. As it left, the train was stoned by an irate mob and some twenty minutes later, a coach has been burned to cinder along with fifty-eight helpless passengers. Who the attackers were and what prompted them to such cruelty are unknown but the rulers of Gujarat promptly decided all <u>Muslims had to be taught a lesson</u>. 'Retaliation' was swift and merciless, some would even say clinical. Over the next few days, several hundred Muslims were killed in a state-wide carnage that is certain to become a part of our 'past that will not pass'" (Underline mine).[2]

After ten years, there has been no closure for the victims of the massacre. The legal procedures have been slow and without any firm resolve to punish the guilty. The Bharatiya Janata Party (BJP) continues to rule the state as it was doing then. Elections have been held and the BJP has won them. There is a feeling of helplessness among the minorities in the state, particularly among the Muslims. One is reminded of another incident that happened before this pogrom in Gujarat. It is the tragedy of Orissa. Rev. Graham Staines[3], an Australian Baptist missionary and his two sons, Timothy and Philip, were burned alive in the district of Keonjhar in Orissa on 23 January, 1999.[4] Later still, in the Kandamal district of Orissa, a riot took place involving the *Hindutva* elements running amok among the Christian tribals. The trigger point was the killing of a Hindu monk, Swami Laxmanananda Saraswati on 23 August, 2008. The retaliation was swift involving looting, burning and raping. This state was also under the joint rule of BJP and BJD (Biju Janta Dal).

---

[2] Varadarajan, Siddharth (Ed.). *Gujarat: The Making of a Tragedy*. New Delhi: Penguin Books India, 2002.

[3] *Ibid.*, p. 3.

[4] *Graham Staines Story*, Web [http://ibsresources.org/index.html, accessed 9 October 2011].

As I stated earlier, closure and resolutions are hard to come by in these incidents. The people who look for resolutions take the platforms of art and literature to find solace and pick up the pieces to move on with life. Recently, three films have been made, these related to Gujarat Tragedy and Communal Violence. These three films, I think, help those who need some solace to move on with life even though these certainly do not put the lid on the tragedy but ultimately point to the uselessness and meaninglessness of such pogroms.

Rahul Dholakia made *Parzania* in 2007, a film said to be inspired by a true story. Cyrus and Shernaz are Parsi – a small community whose ancestors migrated to India from Persia, the present day Iran. They live in a middle class housing complex with their son Parzan (10 years) and their daughter Dilshad (7 years). Many Muslim families and few Hindu families live in that housing complex. Soon after the train incident in Godhra on 27 February, this housing complex is attacked. The Muslims are identified and killed and their belongings are burned. Cyrus is out to his work. Shernaz (the name sounds Muslim) runs away with her two children. In the chase, she loses her son Parzan. The film narrates their ordeal of finding out their son, a search still open after seven years.[5]

The visuals establish the tapestry and the background of what happens. The film proves that the Bajrang Dal, a Hindutva group, wear a saffron head-cloth while the volunteers of the Vishwa Hindu Parishad have a black head-cloth. Before the housing complex where Cyrus and his family live is attacked, these volunteers mark houses and residences with saffron flags signifying that these houses belong to Hindus, and consequently are to be considered safe and not to be attacked. There are dialogues in which some of these Hindutva elements show their annoyance as they think that the Muslims living in India have been supporting the Pakistani cricket team, etc.

The visuals establish that the police have been bribed with liquors. The kerosene and petrol containers have been stored and have been systematically supplied to the volunteers to use against the Muslims. The *tilak*, the *'Om'* sign, the *namabali cloth*, the *trishuls* [for these

---

[5] The Back Cover of the DVD of *Parzania*, produced by the Jorden Electronics, 257 Palika Bazar, Connaught Place, New Delhi, 2007.

words see note 7], the *swords* have been used to strike at the Muslims. Allan, an American researcher on Gandhi, is stunned to see this madness and looks for an answer while trying to help Shernaz and Cyrus find their son Parzan. Mahatma Gandhi's philosophy of non-violence and the importance of the spinning wheel are put in contrast to whatever is happening in Gujarat.

The Human Rights Commission is constituted. But will truth ever be found? The people, the victims who are there for the deposition of their stories, are afraid of the backlashes. Shernaz opens up and tells the commission the truth. The others follow. Cyrus as per his religious teachings undertakes a fast for nine days to purify himself so that he can find his son. He has a vision – he sees his son dead and passed onto another world.

Cyrus comes back after his purification rites. He is still looking for his son after seven years. He is still looking for an answer to the question as to what his son and others have done to be punished in such a manner. He will wait for an answer. The film ends with no closure. Parzania is a world made of the sweets, the chocolates and the ice creams imagined by Parzan. That world has been shattered. The people of India have been shattered, broken to pieces. Parzania, the imaginative land of chocolate and ice-cream, has been destroyed – India has been destroyed. The film broadly but sharply sketches and represents the deep divide between the two communities. One is left with a feeling that nothing will be able to bring them close. Instead of having an end, the film creates intensity in the viewers, a desire to move on looking for Parzan with a saddened hope.

Firaaq, a film made in 2009, by the actress Nandita Das, is based on the shattered lives of those who survived the pogrom. *Firaaq* is "an Urdu word that means both separation and quest. *Firaaq* is a work of fiction based on a thousand true stories. It is an ensemble film that takes place over a 24 hour period. A month after the worst of the violence is over. The film traces the emotional journeys of 'ordinary people' –

some who were victims, some perpetrators and some who watched silently. *Firaaq* explores their relationships as they experience many fierce and delicate emotions of fear and prejudice, guilt and revenge, trust and betrayal and a loss of innocence that wounds the soul forever".[6]

Firaaq tells several stories of lives who survived the massacre and about those who are trying to pick up pieces and attempt to create a sense of life in them. The film begins in a graveyard where several trucks bring a large number of dead bodies for burial. Among the dead there is a Hindu woman. Indeed dead have no religion, no gender and no caste. Munira and her husband return to their burned house and make a new beginning. They are irritated and scared by the constant presence of the police. They are, particularly Munira, haunted by a broach which resembles that of her Hindu friend. She constantly questions her about who set fire on their home. To this her friend keeps quiet and tells Munira what would happen if she should come to know the name of the arsonist, what's more she is not aware of the identity. Munira has found the broach among the burned rubbish in their house. This broach resembles her friend's broach. This redoubles her doubt that her friend knows the culprit and was present during the incident.

Samir, full name Samir Arshad Sheik, a Muslim married to a Hindu woman, is in great pain with his own identity since he is considered a Hindu as his name Samir is also a Hindu name. This has created a kind of cover on his identity. He also once uses the surname of his wife, Desai. Samir decides to move to Delhi where the vastness of the city will hide his identity and he will be able to make a new beginning. However, Samir picks up his courage and discloses his identity with firm conviction and decides not to leave Ahmedabad. On looking back, he reasons out his inability to clearly declare his identity as a Muslim; now he says that he did not have the balls to do that. He now does that in the most adverse situation. He says to his wife that he felt good by clearly telling all that he was a Muslim and he was Samir Arshad Sheikh. Indeed, a resurrection of the self in difficult times.

The story of Aarti, again a life in dissonance and pain, is a story concerning the acceptance of what her inner self has been constantly

---

[6] The Back Cover of the DVD of *Firaaq*, produced by the Eagle Home Entertainment Pvt., J-12 Jangpura Ext., New Delhi, 2009.

telling her to do. Aarti is a Hindu housewife whose members are deeply Hindutva minded. The husband of Aarti, during the massacre has been found looting shops (caught in camera). He is a short-tempered person. Aarti is haunted by the image of a woman (presumably Muslim) who requested her to open the door to save herself from a chasing crowd. She did not. Later Aarti meets a small Muslim boy. She takes this boy home and gives him a Hindu name 'Mohan' and covers his identity medal (*tabiz*) underneath his shirt. Aarti hides him in his kitchen, the last thing a Hindu woman would do to make her house impure. Aarti has been burning her hand bit by bit to understand the agony and the pain undergone by the woman who was chased.

She has also applied turmeric to heal the burned spots. Mohan tells her how his mother was tortured and killed and how in the chaos he lost his father. He is still looking for him. Mohan sees how Aarti's husband beats her. He also asks her whether she has also been burnt. Mohan quietly leaves Aarti's house and moves on and takes shelter in a camp while still looking for his father. Aarti takes a bold step by going outside and leaving behind her torturous house. The light brightens the images signifying the emancipation of Aarti and her gained freedom. In another episode Munira's husband gets killed by the police. This happens when he and other young Muslim men are planning to take revenge and accidentally a gun is shot by a mentally ill person who happens to be a Muslim and a part of their team. The police then chase the members and Munira's husband is killed by a person dropping a slab on him from an upper floor as he is resting below after a long chase-run.

The last story concerns Khan Saab, a Hindustani classical musician. People, both Hindus and Muslims, used to assemble in his sitting room and he would perform for them regularly. His servant watches television habitually and is aware of the reason why the usual audience in the evening has dramatically dropped since the last month. The old Khan Saab is unaware of what is happening, leave alone how deep the divide is between Hindus and Muslims; he watches the news as his servant has been taken to a hospital to be treated for a cut in his finger. Khan Saab realises that Hindu people are rioting only after watching the television news, and is visibly disturbed with the communal divide. He is in distress. His doctor friend (a Hindu), Aarti, (who in the meanwhile has reconciled with her husband, who has discarded his Hindu fanatic attitude), have decided to come back again to attend Khan Saab's *mazleesh* [musical meeting] The environment brightens up and the melody flows from the voice of Khan Saab. These four stories interplay throughout *Firaaq*; they proceed towards some sort of resurrection for these characters from the gloomy lighting and very tight images signifying suppression. The film moves towards bright, broad and spacious images. The pain and distress still remain. The closure is not there, but lives move on with hope.

The third film in discussion is *Mr. and Mrs. Iyer*. The story is of a journey that Meenakshi Iyer undertakes with her infant son alone from a hill station in North Bengal to Kolkata, where her husband would receive them. The anxious parents of Meenakshi find Raja Chaudhury, a family friend, who is also travelling on the same bus. The ordeal starts when the roads are blocked and everything is out of gear as the riot between Hindus and Muslims breaks out in a nearby area and is spreading like wild fire. Meenakshi and Raja try to find a safe place and try to reach somehow Kolkata by train. During this struggle, Meenakshi, a Tamil Brahmin, discovers that Raja is a Muslim and his actual name is Jahangir Chowdhury. Raja (a Hindu name) is his pet name. They reach Kolkata safe. Meenakshi and Raja come to know each other and develop a bond (even though for a short while) beyond their religious identities.

The film starts with a shot of the passengers in the bus. All kinds of people: Sikhs, Tamils, Bengalis, and others are travelling in the bus. A group of young boys and girls are singing and dancing – enjoying the ride. The bus stops as the road is blocked. The Hindutva militants enter the bus and look for Muslims. They are represented with the known symbols of *saffron clothes, namabali, trishuls, tilaks*[7] and fierce-looking faces. They are uttering the usual anti-Muslim rhetoric such as Muslims should go to Pakistan, and they (Muslims) are staying here and multiplying.

---

[7] *Saffron* is a colour associated with Hindu religion. It, in most cases, represents the disinterestedness in worldly affairs. *Namabali* is a Hindu piece of cloth, again mostly of saffron colour, with the names of the gods and of the goddess printed on it. *Trishul* is a kind of a trident used by gods, particularly Shiva and the goddess. *Tilak* is a vermilion mark put on the forehead.

A passenger identifies an old Muslim couple. The old man is taken away from the bus; his wife gives him his spectacles and denture. A girl realises what will happen to the old man and tries to stop him from being taken away. She is slapped and falls unconscious. The old Muslim lady, realising the incoming danger to the life of her husband, tries to stop them from taking him away. The Hindutva men take her away too. A young man is forced to open his pants to prove whether or not he is a Hindu, as Muslim males are circumcised. The other terrified passengers convince the Hindutva militants by stating 'Hum Saab Hindu Hai' (we are all Hindus). Raja is uncomfortable as these militants are approaching all passengers and enquiring about their religion. Meenakshi states that she is Meenakshi Iyer and Raja is her husband, Mr. Iyer. In the meanwhile, the old Muslim's spectacles and denture are spread over not very far from the bus, thus signifying that the couple have been killed.

During a conversation Raja tells the police that an old Muslim couple have been killed, the police curtly reply saying that they would investigate. Later, Meenkshi and Raja witness a Muslim being butchered. Meenkshi's comment is that it is so easy to kill a person. In this film, Raja, a wild life photographer, is portrayed as a very caring and cultured person. This is quite contrary to the image of the Muslims that the Hindutva elements portray. Aparna Sen, the director, simply demolishes all through the film the stereotype images of the Muslims and creates a character endowed with impeccable integrity. Meenakshi goes through this painful journey of discovering this wonderful Muslim co-traveller and develops a very soft corner for him. She is left with only the photographs of this journey leading to her awareness.

These three films, based on the communal violence of Gujarat 2002, have opened windows on human relationships before, during and after the Gujarat violence. The identity of religion deeply defines the human relationship in the context of Gujarat, and broadly of India particularly in *Mr. and Mrs. Iyer*.

The Hindutva movement has begun in the pre-independence days through the works of Vinayak Damodar Savarkar. The Vishwa Hindu Parishad (VHP), the Rastriya Sayamsevak Sang (RSS), the Bajrang Dal and some groups have been galvanising the citizens, particularly the Hindus, to form a solid base for the creation of a Hindurastra (a Hindu nation) in which the minorities, such as Muslims and Christians, will be permitted to live at the pleasure of the majority and should remain as second class citizens. The Bharatiya Janta Party (BJP), the political wing of this movement has been doing its job at the political front, such as forming regional and central governments strengthening the agenda of Hindutva. In 2002, during the massacre and thereafter, the BJP was in power and permitted various groups of the Hindutva movement to run amok during the February pogrom.

There has been distribution of *swords*, *trishuls* [tridents], *lathis* [staves] and *dharias* [iron rods]. There have been rituals performed by the Trishul Diksha Samarohs (TDS) in various places of Gujarat before the riot. All these under the nose of Gujarat law and order force – the police. There have been as seen in *Firaaq* and *Parzania* distribution of petrol, kerosene and gas cylinders. These were liberally used to burn houses, shops and dead bodies after people were killed. All these traditional Hindu arms and weapons and the use of fire and inflammable liquid create a pattern. In the films here discussed, no killing takes place by guns or pistols though these must have been available in a modern society.

The *trishul*, *swords*, *dharias* and *lathis* are the weapons used by Hindu gods for their *Sanhara* (annihilation) of the enemy or devils. The Hindutva groups inspired by their own gods use the same weapons for the *Sanhara* of the current day enemy or *other self* as told by V.D. Savarkar, the Muslims.[8] One may look at the various images of the Hindu gods abounding in various places and platforms. They are in the posture of *Sanhara* brandishing and using the weapons stated above. The image of the Hindu religion as secular, inclusive and broad-based somehow is not projected as should have been. In reality, the peaceful and tolerant aspect of this great religion is being portrayed less and less as the "militant" Hinduism has filled in the vacuum. The inspiration for the cadres of the Hindutva group as depicted in the films comes from the current day images of the gods. The cadres see Muslims, Christians, Adivasis [tribals] and other minorities as the devils or impure who are

---

[8] Sharma, Jyotirmaya. *Hindutva: Exploring the Idea of Hindu Nationalism*. New Delhi: Penguin Books India, 2006, p. 137.

to be either annihilated or co-opted. When the co-opting strategies fail, the only option left is annihilation.

Question also arises as to why so much burning or the use of fire was going during the riot. There could be two reasons for this: i) to erase all the evidences of the atrocities committed, so that the perpetrators could not be tracked down and also the dead bodies could not be identified; and ii) to purify the dead, setting their souls free and thereby bringing them back to the Hindu folds. There have been clues in both *Firaaq* and *Parzania* about the intention of the Muslims taking revenge for the atrocities committed against them. *Firaaq* and *Parzania* produce a feeling among the audience that the closure has to happen. Without the closure, the wound will not heal. *Mr. and Mrs. Iyer* tells us that we need to discover the *other* and must look for opportunities for such eventualities.

The Sangh Parivar group (including the Rashtriya Swayamsevak Sangh, the Vishwa Hindu Parishad, Bajran Dal, the BJP and Abhinov Bharat) has their foundational aim given by Vinayak Damodar Savarkar and later by some articulate individuals like Madhav Sadashiv Golwalkar purposing to establish a Hindurastra.[9] These groups have embarked on this agenda by adopting various methods. What has been depicted by these three films is the process of ethnically cleansing the Indian nation from the impurities (Muslims, Christians and other minorities). Such violence is to continue if Hindurastra is to be established. These films are depictions of the symptoms only. Hence, there is a problem about the image of Hindutva as a peaceful, secular, tolerant and diverse (inclusive) one. The deeper one looks at the icons and images of its gods and goddesses, in its folk stories, in its epics, or one considers the rise of Hindutva with the high priests like Savarkar and Golwalkar, one can see violence, killings, bloodbath, wars and its protagonists involving themselves in *Kuta-yuddha* tactics [unrighteous war].[10] One therefore, cannot overlook this aspect of Hindutva. And one can conclude that the path undertaken by the groups of Sangh Parivar in order to establish Hindurastra is certainly steeped into violence. The

---

[9] Sharma, Jyotirmaya, *op.cit.*, p. 7.
[10] Gittinger, Juli. "Saffron Terror: Splinter or Symptom?", in *Economic and Political Weekly*, vol. XLVI No. 37, 10 September 2011, pp. 22-25.

ideology decisively points out to this path, quite contrary to the inclusive and secular image that we have had in the past.

Another aspect of the violence that one encounters in these films is the raping of women. This is also found quite often in many other violent incidents that happen regularly. Women represent the dignity and purity of any community in Indian context. It could be the same for other nations and communities also. During the partition of India in 1947, in the Punjab province many Sikh males killed their own daughters and wives so that they would not be violated. Therefore, if one wants to hurt a community or a group, rape is the weapon that is used. The violence, in the form of rape, as depicted in these three films is no exception.

The tragedy of Gujarat happened in 2002 and is still in the news. The related cases are being heard in courts. The victims are still looking for justice and thereby a closure to their wounds. It is not happening now. It may not be happening in the near future. The literature, including films, fiction and different kinds of analysis, based on this tragedy indicate this numbness and pain. The three films of *Parzania*, *Firaaq* and *Mr. & Mrs. Iyer* are part of the unsolved tragedy and pain.

[Reference Note]

We give a literal translation of the Hindutva groups mentioned in the article.

Vishwa Hindu Parishad: General Hindu Assembly.

Ras(h)triya S(w)ayamsevak Sang(h): National, of the Same Colour, Same Hindu Identity, Follower.

Bharatiya Janta Party: Indian People Party.

Trishul(a) Diksha Samaroh: Trident, Convocation.

Sang(h) Parivar: United (Group), Family. It refers to several associated groups, among them the Bajran Dal and the Abhinav Bharat

Bajran Dal: Strong (Thunderbolt), group.

Abhinav Bharat: Modern (Innovative) India. The society has been founded by Vinayak Damodar Savarkar.

They Kill Kittens Like This, Don't They?

Alessandro Monti

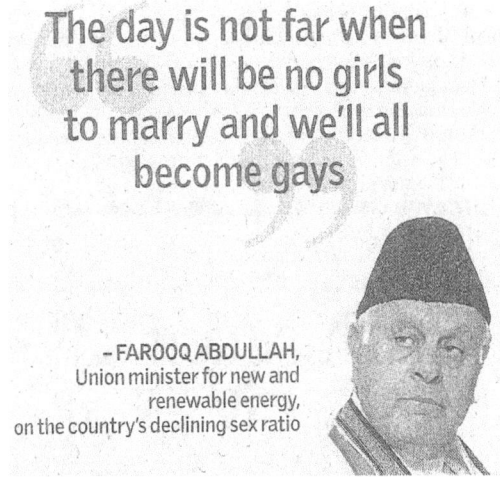

The day is not far when there will be no girls to marry and we'll all become gays

– FAROOQ ABDULLAH,
Union minister for new and
renewable energy,
on the country's declining sex ratio

The Times of India, Lucknow Edition, 13 April 2011.

In the shocking scene that opens the film *Matrubhoomi* (*The Land of Women*, 2003) a peasant drowns in a cauldron full of milk and water his newborn baby girl. Similar malpractices acting traditionally as a rustic and homemade control which concerns the female sex ratio are quite common in Indian villages, especially in socially different areas such as Punjab, Haryana, Bihar, Gujarat and Rajasthan. This kind of killings is still witnessed in a short news item which appeared recently on *The Times of India*, Lucknow Edition, 5 April 2011,

Infanticide in this village of 13 girls?

Vimal Bhatia | TNN

Jaisalmer: The recent census showed alarming details about skewed sex ratio. An incident in Rajasthan's Jaisalmer district can serve as an eyeopener.

A family quietly went home after a baby girl was born at a hospital in the district's Devra village, 80km from Jaisalmer, notorious for girl child killings.

The baby was declared dead after a few hours and was buried on March 31.

Villagers complained to the district authorities that the family killed the baby following which a case was registered. The baby's mother is the only woman in this village of 300 families to have got married in 106 years. There are only 13 girls, all below 10 years, in the village.

The citation epitomises to the point the basic premises behind the starting story-line in the film – that is, the extinction of girls in villages and rural areas, given the recurrent infanticides. However, things are rather worse than that, since the rustic dispatching of an unwelcome girl has been widely replaced by sex-determination and select abortion (or foeticide). Apparently *Matrubhoomi* deals with pre-modern issues, in a scenery of total backwardness prior to the advent of the diagnostic machines. As a matter of fact its archaic dimension is suggested by a *post quem* status – the extinction of women within the village. In its representation of a time afterwards, the film exposes the core of gender bias which still haunts Indian society, notwithstanding its transition to modernity.

The burdening daughter is the obvious reason behind female infanticides and foeticides – even if the film does not consider the causes behind these malpractices. It rather anticipates as a warning what will happen when all women will be killed in India. As such *Matrubhoomi* might be viewed as it were a post-catastrophe dystopia, one following ideally a book on the plight of women in India and China (*Quand les femmes auront disparu. L'élimination des filles en Inde et en Asie*).[1] So, the background village in *Matrubhoomi* is metaphorically

---

[1] That is, *When no more Women Will Be Left. Killing Daughters in India and in Asia*, Manier, Bénédicte. Paris: La Découverte, 2006.

correlated to the whole Indian nation, whose doom it anticipates in a rather gruesome way.

As such the village in the film concentrates on a handful of issues (subordination of women, extensive rape, domestic violence, casteism and communal violence) which are magnified if one shifts to a general overview of Indian society. Sticking to women, it would be highly proficient to isolate at least a couple of major factors leading to this kind of mass murder against them, either infanticide or foeticide. In more recent times it is associated with the rising and affluent (high) middle-class, in particular among the so-called urbanites. They plan births according to their ascent to the heaven of consumerism and recur again and again to echography and subsequent female foeticide (Manier 2006: 57-64). Ultrasonic determination concerning the sex of the foetus is also quickly spreading in the villages and in the rural areas – there they rub shoulders with the more traditional techniques of post-birth killings.

Consequently, the initial drowning scene in *Matrubhoomi* acquires a two-pronged determination of time, since it can be analysed from a contemporary perspective (one associated with change in society); however it intimates at the same time continuity with an archaic past. Behind the cauldron of watered milk lurks a time-honoured metaphor, whose meaning is to expose catachrestically the ruinous nature of women and in particular of daughters. It should be remembered that a Sanskrit paronomasia for a daughter defines her as a *duhita*, that is, one who wastes the resources of the family, from *duh*, milk.[2] The Indian version of the Greek myth of Pandora (the woman *gaster*, stomach, whose greediness devours the reserves of food) may be easily spotted for instance in the novel *Gauri*, also known as *The Old Woman and the Cow*, by Mulk Raj Anand (1960). When Gauri has come back home after leaving her husband, "The cow, Chandari, also moved and waved her head to greet her long lost sister, who had tended her before she went away as a bride; and she nearly kicked the pitcher as she strained to get free to come to Gauri".[3]

---

[2] Uma, A. *Woman and her Family*. New Delhi: Sterling, 1989, p. 3.
[3] Anand, Mulk Raj. *Gauri (The Old Woman and the Cow)*. New Delhi: Arnold-Heinemann, 1981 (1960), p. 104.

The metaphorical sisterhood or propinquity between the family cow and the young woman introduces an issue which will be dealt with further on in my article – now the domestic equation cow-docile or gentle wife is crucial ("Gauri is like a cow, very gentle and very good", p. 11; "Chachi, Gauri had the reputation of being as gentle as a cow in her village", p. 41). Of course docility means submission, or her role as a domestically "trained" (an adjective used in *matrimonials*) useful commodity. Sexual docility is the basic requisite imposed to a woman in *Matrubhoomi*, whereas the metaphor concealed in the passage of the cow and the pitcher illustrates how she is a constant threat to the family welfare and to the family bonds. This shared reference to women identity constitutes de facto the conceptual correlative which instructs the archaic techniques of disposing female newborns off, prior to the "modern possibility" allowing parents to take advantage of pre-natal ultrasonographic sex determination.

In the rural setting of *Matrubhoomi*, the economy of gender appraisal which leads parents to kill daughters partakes more of extreme issues concerning survival rather than emphasising the wish to achieve or maintain an upward position in the social scale. The basic problem behind this malpractice regards the yielding of a dowry on the part of the family of the bride, plus the incessant flow of gifts and cash, as requested according to custom.[4] People can even pun on the matter and interpret the abbreviation "SD" (Sex determination, referring to the sex of the foetus) as "Solution to Dowry" (Manier 2006: 39). More idioms concerning the dichotomy at birth between a male and a female might be quoted here – one is however enough: a newborn baby boy is referred to as a *muffat lal* (a free boy), whereas a baby girl is a *ayee chuki*, enough of coming (Patel 2007: 150). These antecedents either pertaining to custom or reasons of domestic economy, constitute the corporate background of *Matrubhoomi*, its proairetic movement towards the development of the story. A further diegetic step involves the referential roles of myth and traditional lexicon within the filmic tradition, from the co-sharing of a wife (as in the *Mahabharata*) to the symbolical reference to milk and cows. That means a double texture of reality, one inside the other.

---

[4] Patel, Tulsi. "The Mindset Behind Eliminating the Female Foetus.", in Tulsi Patel (Ed.), *Sex-Selective Abortion in India*. New Delhi: Sage, 2007, pp. 164-168.

The archaic dimension of the tale (in which the initial scene of the drowning assumes a ritualistic value) suggests a status of congealed time – here the repetition of a gesture transcends the mere formal significance but entails the extreme maintaining of a corporate domestic identity, whose primary agency is the family and its honour, values which imply the *duhita-like*, or Pandora-like, imagining of the woman. Consequently, the village in the film stands across two time-frames: it belongs both to the timeless sphere of Indian culture and simultaneously anticipates virtually a near future to come, but already a present in being. Of course I refer specifically to the post-2011 census alarm in the growing unbalanced ratio between men and women in India.

If one considers *Matrubhoomi* a projected vision of the days to come, it should be viewed and assessed as a post-catastrophe narration, one outside the path of history but instructing patterns of myth instead of representing a society in movement. The collapsing frame entails then a nation without women, a gay farmhouse as intimated by a minister – after the initial scene of drowning the film focuses progressively on a cross-dressing nautch dance, a hilarious viewing of pornographic cassettes, and finally sodomy with a cow. This scenery lays totally bare the regressive corporate identity of the village (the so-called very heart of India), whose community only includes sex-starved single men. A bedtrick follows, when a marriage is arranged in the village involving a boy from a nearby community. Of course the bride-boy pretends to be a girl and dresses as such, but his true identity is disclosed during the matrimonial rites. This episode concludes the first macro-sequence in the film.

Henceforward, the focus is shifted to a high-caste family – a widowed father and five unmarried brothers, plus a young male servant of lower caste who cooks almost uneatable food. Once again, the narration switches to a traditional mythical tale, one mixing together *Sakuntala* and the *Mahabharata*, casteism and the practice of bride-price. The first sequence includes the appearance of a maiden in the wood. At the very break of dawn the family or village priest spots a beautiful young woman washing herself in the river. He follows her to a cottage among the trees, where she lives in concealment with her father. This scenery might remember *Sakuntala* and the Sanskrit idyllic meeting of love, but it turns quickly to a nightmare. The girl is given off by her father to the whole upper caste family for a nice price.

Bride price indicates a process of de-sanskristisation, since it goes against the practice of the dowry and falls back on exchange marriage and bride wealth marriage (Patel 2007: 162). The difference in status between the bride giver and the receiver deconstructs the ritual notion of the gift of a virgin (*kanyadan*), by replacing a mere financial interest for it. In *Matrubhoomi* price bride (also implied in the initial bedtricking marriage) is used by the *dehati* (peasant) father of the young woman as the means to improve his social status, from the countryside to town. Thus the ritual exchange involving two households, within a possibility of hypergamy, is reduced to an individual act of selling. In the upside-vision of the film a daughter may boost her father to wealth, instead of depleting his resources.

However, the shared co-bride is reduced to a passive condition of domestic and sexual exploitation and servitude. This joint marriage may be reminiscent of the *Mahabharata* and of Draupadi, but it turns out to be a nightmarish gang-raping, since the rule is a co-husband every night (the father included). A useful commodity, the shared wife is downgraded, not metaphorically, to a mere and exploited provider of food (the men enjoy at least good fare) and sex. Her condition of domestic slavery qualifies the film on the fringes of feudal drama, such as *Ankur* (*The Seedling*, 1973) and above all *Nishant* (*When Night Comes*, 1978), the latter a film which shares with *Matrubhoomi* the final slaughter of the village landlords. These references endorse the composite narrative structure of the film, whose story should be understood in fracturing sequences of oppression and patriarchal tyranny.

The seeds of domestic violence grow into murder, when the youngest son, the only decent person in the family, is killed by his brothers, with the complicity of the father, out of sheer malevolent jealousy, because of his kind and human relationship with the unhappy wife. This murder marks the starting of communal violence – in fact the horrified wife tries to escape with the help of the young servant. They are easily found out by the brothers, who kill the boy and take the runaway woman back home. She is clapped down in the stable, so as to enforce docility on her. Now she is virtually equated to a cow, in a punishment which frames her identity of fallen woman. It is crucial to the symbolic purpose the gaze which a coterminous cow addresses her, perhaps to indicate awareness of guilt and reproach. This scene should be confronted with what happens in *Amar* (1954), when the ravished milkmaid goes back to her hut and the family cow looks at her, in a reflection of the sense of guilt which is racking the woman.

However, the reduction of the rebellious wife to a tamed cow marks a decisive turning point in the atmosphere of violence the film is imbued with. It moves the perspective from domesticity to communalism, since to revenge the death of the servant the low-caste peasants start to gang-rape surreptitiously the woman on their own. So the body of the woman becomes the arena in which upper and lower castes clash, in a full and tremendous transition from corporate domesticity to inter-castal conflict. Continuous raping leads consequentially to pregnancy, then to communal opposed revendications of fatherhood, a further seminal value in Indian culture, and even in the notion of family honour. Ironically enough a baby-girl is born, but her birth does not constitute necessarily an investment for the future: the enraged peasants slaughter both priest and landlords while the mother leaves the village with the new boy servant.

A faint image of hope, for the days to come, even if the film shows a crumbling-down society deep in blood and dissolution. The line of difference between paradox and reality seems to be very thin given the composite focus on female infanticide, rape, domestic violence and casteism. A further thrust against social custom is cast through the father of the harassed wife. Its cynical behaviour denounces the non-values of the rising urban middle class, whose acquired social status is uniquely grounded on money and greed. As a final asset, *Matrubhoomi* makes devastating havoc about the rhetoric of India as the country of the youth. That might also be, but after extended sex determination.

Appendix

It includes a few articles concerning child sex ratio in Uttar Pradesh, along with others on women's inequality and poorer literacy. The unchecked proliferation of diagnostic and ultrasonic centres has further modified the CSR, both in rural areas and urban centres. For more detailed information see "Comment les filles disparaissent" (Manier 2006). The 2011 Census in India has contributed to highlight not only the issue of the CSR, but also focused on the general discrimination against girl-children. To conclude, it should be noticed that sex determination is the anteroom of female foeticide, or sex-selective abortion. Outside urban centres it is closely associated with the officially forbidden practice of dowry and bride price. Another cause concerns culture norms such as those against inter-caste marriages or unions within the same *gotra* or lineage. In cities and towns ultrasonic and diagnostic centres or clinic take charge of sex determination and female foeticide, for an average price of around 2000 rupees. This trend mainly regards the upper layers of society, to be roughly identified with the rising urban middle classes and affluent farmers, especially from Punjab or Haryana. More articles follow, not only on sex determination, but on the general conditions of women and girls.

'In 20 yrs, 20% more men than women'

Sex-Selective Abortions & Male Bias Will Be Main Reason, Says Study

Kounteya Sinha | TNN

New Delhi: India will have 20% more men than women in the next two decades, thanks to sex-selective abortion and craze for male child in some states, according to a new study.

Conducted by Dr Therese Hesketh and co-authors from the UCL Centre for International Health and Development, London, and published in the Canadian Medical Association Journal on Tuesday, the study says easy access to sex-selective abortions, has led to significant imbalances in the male/ female population in China, India and South Korea.

The sex ratio at birth (SRB) — the number of boys born to every 100 girls — is consistent in human populations, where about 105 males are born to every 100 females. The study says, in India there are also marked regional differences in SRB.

Incompleteness of birth registration makes it difficult to accurately calculate SRB. However, using the closely related ratio of boys to girls under the age of six, it is found that there are several states in the north and west such as Punjab, Delhi and Gujarat that have sex ratios as high as 125.

In the south and east, several states — such as Kerala and Andhra Pradesh — have sex ratios of around 105. "India is now reported to have an SRB of around 113, which is

GENDER BENDER

down from a peak of around 116," Dr Hesketh said.

According to the study, there are already laws forbidding foetal sex determination and sex-selective abortion in China, India and South Korea.

"South Korea has only enforced the law strongly. In China and India, sex-selective abortion is still carried out with impunity by medical personnel, usually qualified doctors, in hospitals and clinics, not in backstreet establishments. This makes the failure of government to enforce the law all the more surprising," the study says.

"A common pattern is that if the first- or second-born are girls, then couples often ensure the second or third child is a boy," its adds.

A consistent pattern in all three countries is the gender of the preceding child. "If the first child is a girl, couples will often sex select to ensure a boy in the second pregnan-

cy especially where low fertility is the norm.

A large study in India showed that for second births with one preceding girl the SRB is 132, and for third births with two previous girls it is 139, while sex ratios where the previous child was a boy are normal," the study explains.

India has 34,012 registered ultra-sound clinics. Earlier, studies have said 5-7 lakh girls a year or 2,000 girls go missing in India daily due to female foeticide. In families, where one girl child already exists, the chances of a second girl being born are as low as 54%. In a family with two female children, the chances of third girl being born is as low as 20%.

The Times of India, Lucknow Edition, 17 March 2011.

'Trend of female foeticide catching up very fast'

Staff Reporter

* 'If 10 lakh abortions done every year, why aren't even 10 doctors punished?'

* 'We should critically question techniques that emerged with aim of finding perfection'

MUMBAI: Urgent and sustained efforts needed to curb female foeticide were discussed at a two-day workshop on "female foeticide: rights of the girl child, problems and solutions," held at the Tata Institute of Social Sciences (TISS) here on Friday and Saturday.

The workshop was organised to mark the National Girl Child Week from January 24 to 31.

"The sex ratio in the country is decreasing at an alarming rate. The educated, upper classes, and upper castes have started the trend of female foeticide, and it is catching up very fast. We should not be surprised if the 2011 census shows the same trend in the tribal areas too," chief chairperson of Men Against Violence and Abuse (MAVA) Harish Sadani said during the workshop. The workshop was jointly organised by the Maharashtra State Social Welfare Board, MAVA, Stree Mukti Sanghatana, and the TISS for members of non-governmental organisations.

Participants and the speakers discussed the evolution of the Pre-Conception and Pre-Natal Diagnostic Techniques (Prohibition of Sex Selection) Act (PCPNDT Act), the provisions and problems in its implementation, lack of awareness in society, and technological innovations to stop female foeticide.

Explaining the history of the development of public health Acts, Kamakshi Bhate, Head of the Preventive and Social Medicine Department in King Edward Memorial Hospital, said Acts such as the PCPNDT and the age of marriage were a result of people's demand.

"Some Acts come into being because the government thinks of them. But some Acts are made due to people's demand. To fight the tendency of sex determination in society, many women's groups, scientists, doctors, and individuals came together in the 1980s to spread awareness about its ill-effects. They demanded legislation against sex determination and pre-selection," Dr. Bhate noted.

Expressing the need for the government to take a proactive role in curbing sex pre-selection, she said doctors needed to be punished severely if they were found to be disobeying the law. "If 10 lakh abortions are done every year, why aren't even 10 doctors punished?" she said, citing studies done by Population First and Laadli.

Vigilance authorities in the government should be made aware of their role. "Many a time, the vigilance authorities themselves don't know what action they have to take. They need to be trained and made aware," she said.

Social activist and academician Chhaya Datar said there should be a collective value system in society, and that a girl child's birth should be valued. "We need to educate doctors and build up their value system so that they do not do things only in accordance with their commercial interests."

There was a need to look at technological developments critically, Dr. Datar said.

"Now there are techniques through which you can filter the X chromosomes and Y chromosomes to ensure that a child of a particular sex is born. All these techniques emerged with the aim of finding perfection. We should question that and stop looking for perfection," she said.

Mr. Sadani pointed out that in parts of western Maharashtra, girls were increasingly being named 'Nakoshi' (unwanted).

"What is it that makes us name our girls 'unwanted'? When we talked to youths in this region, they said girls do not understand how to deal in society. I think we should work on this patriarchal attitude and teach youths to respect women, their bodies, and their contribution in chores," he said.

The workshop also discussed the effects of "Silent Observer," a technological innovation used in four districts of Maharashtra to monitor and control the growing incidence of sex pre-determination.

"The sex ratio in Kolhapur has improved substantially after the implementation of this project," said Girish Lad, inventor of "Silent Observer." He said the machines were installed around two years ago.

"According to the 2001 census data, the child sex ratio [between 0-6 years] was 839 in Kolhapur. In December 2010, it was 901. There is a sizeable decrease in the number of female foeticides in Kolhapur as the doctors have started fearing governmental action. They know that there is data available to act against them," he said. Mr. Lad added that the machines helped gather valuable statistical data that was otherwise not available with the government machinery.

The Hindu, Lucknow Edition, 31 January 2011.

Most people feel awareness is the key to stem female foeticide

Women in state make sense of census

SMITA KUMAR

Patna, April 1: India's plunging sex ratio has set off the alarm and to make matters worse, the figures revealed by the 2011 census reveals it is the lowest in 50 years.

With the decrease in sex ratio in Bihar as well, women in the state feel more awareness should be created among the people, especially in rural areas.

According to the provisional data released by the census of India on Thursday, Bihar's population has risen to 10.38 crore in 2011 from 8.29 crore in 2001. On the other hand, the sex ratio has reduced to 916 from

919 in 2001.

The sex ratio is defined as the number of females for every 1000 males.

Kakkashan Parveen, the chairperson of Bihar State Women's Commission, said: "This is something to be thought over. Awareness should be created or else a day will come when no girl will be left to be married to a boy. How can a society be imagined without girls? Girls and boys are complementary to each other." Parveen added: "Use of ultrasound machines should be stopped and tabs should be put on doctors."

Tanvi Sinha of Darbhanga House, Patna University

who is pursuing a postgraduate degree in economics, said: "It is necessary to create awareness. People, especially in rural areas, should be made aware of the importance of girls in society. How can a home exist with only boys and no girls? How would it look?"

Sinha is surprised to see the dip in the sex ratio and that too in Nitish's regime when girls are being taken care of.

Sinha said: "The economic standard of the people is rising and perceptions are changing. Under such circumstances how can the sex ratio go down? People should realise girls are no longer con-

sidered burden and parents should never think that investing on them is not practical. Successful stories of women must be narrated to make people aware of their importance."

Manju Singh, a member of the board of directors, Lions Club of Patna Favourite, also echoed similar sentiments.

Singh said: "This should be strongly highlighted at the government level. The reduction in the sex ratio should be put up in the form of slogans on big hoardings."

Singh said: "People should be told how their mindset is affecting the society. There should be no discrimi-

nation between a boy and a girl child."

Singh added: "Doctors too should not promote use of ultrasound machines for determining the sex of the foetus. It is illegal and is one of the reasons behind decrease in the sex ratio."

Namita Singh, zonal chairperson, Lions Club District 322-E, said: "The important thing is awareness. Until and unless people are made aware the ratio would plummet further. People should realise if the ratio keeps on decreasing a day would arrive come when marriages will be next to impossible. Moreover, a society cannot be imagined without girls."

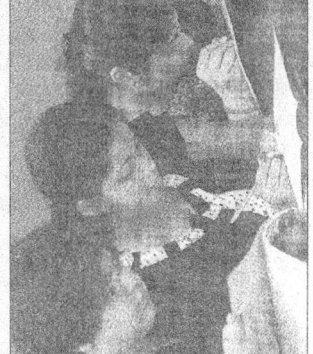

ALARM BELL

The Telegraph, Calcutta (Bihar, Patna Edition), 2 April 2011.

The index of inequality

Do the preliminary census findings confirm that India is united by discrimination against girl-children?

RAVINDER KAUR

FIRST the good news: the overall sex ratio improved from 933 in 2001 to 940 in 2011. There are more women in the Indian population than there were ten years ago. The bad news: there are even fewer girls in the 0-6 age group then there were in 2010. The number went down from 927 in 2001 to 914 in 2011 — a decline of 13 points.

While the perennial question — why don't Indians want daughters — continues to stare us in the face, we need to dissect the provisional child sex ratio figures released by the census commissioner a little carefully to understand the implications.

One positive trend that may go unnoticed in the swirling sea of declines in 24 out of our 35 states/UTs is the improvement in many of the forever guilty northern states — especially Punjab and Haryana. Chandigarh and Delhi, the two much maligned cities, have also shown improvement even though Delhi's — by only one point — hardly calls for celebration. But there is improvement in Himachal Pradesh as also in Gujarat and Tamil Nadu; the latter two are in many ways similar to the northern states. Haryana and Punjab at 830 and 846 still remain states with the worst sex ratios and with J&K joining them, continue to contribute a large share of the country's female deficit, but their upward movement finally should make us take heart.

How about the rest of the coun-

may be improving, the rest of the country is resolutely marching on the path of daughter elimination, continuing trends that began as early as 1971 in some states. It is difficult to explain why north-eastern (and largely tribal) states such as Nagaland, Manipur, Sikkim and Tripura should be showing further and large declines from 1991 and 2001 figures. Other eastern states, Assam and Meghalaya, also show smaller but definite declines. States in this part of the country are generally taken to be more female friendly than the rest of India. And even though most of them continue to have above normal sex ratios (higher than 950) the declines need to be taken as warning signals. West Bengal and Orissa have also continued their 2001 downward trend. Another shocker is the continuing dips in the central Indian tribal states — Jharkhand and Chhatisgarh have declined and so has the hill state of Uttarakhand. STs, as a social group, have had robust sex ratios even though there was a decline between 1991-2001, from 985 to 973. The declines in both the north-eastern and central Indian states, states with tribal populations, means that ST ratios are likely to fall further. Then there are the outliers: A huge drop of 78 points in J&K? And small UTs like Dadra and Nagar Haveli, Daman and Diu have dived by 66 and 16 points respectively.

Can there be one common explanation as to why child sex ratios have been dipping around the country for several decades? Dra-

guage and culture, kinship and marriage, wheat growing and rice growing areas, lower and higher castes, nomadic, tribal and hill people — are we now simply united by our desire to get rid of our daughters?

Unfortunately, the census has as yet not published the critical sex *ratio at birth* (SRB) figures for 2011, that is, answers to the census question: children born, by sex, in the year immediately preceding the census. This ratio will tell us whether the promising signs of a turnaround shown by the sample registration system (SRS) data are corroborated across the country. If the sex ratio at birth for 2011 does show an improvement, then there are two — good and bad news — conclusions to be drawn: sex selective abortions may have reduced

UMMI RAHEH SHANKER

leading to further attrition of girl children up to age six (and perhaps higher). Many rich states like Punjab and poor states like Madhya Pradesh show higher girl child mortality. Madhya Pradesh continues to record cases of female infanticide.

There is also an alternate explanation. The statistic on the sex ratio, 0-6 years, in 2011, is actually an average of sorts of the SRB in the previous seven years. These seven years are centred in 2007, and if there has been an improving trend then the 2004-2010, average of 914 means a higher number for SRB for 2010. The Census 2001 number for SRB was 906, that is, the census SRB in 2010 will most likely be in the high 920s, possibly higher. So while the child sex ratio shows a decline, the birth of girls

sus data reflects the trend upwards in the SRS data. This would be reason for hope that the trend perceived at the tail end of the last decade could become long-lasting.

But to return to the million dollar question on everybody's mind — why does a growing India continue to discriminate against girls? Interestingly, we are not alone in this — China, growing faster than us has a worse problem while rich countries like South Korea have only recently managed to get normal sex ratios at birth. New work by French demographer Christophe Guilmoto shows that the malady may be spreading to other parts of Asia — Vietnam, Singapore, Armenia, Albania, Azerbaijan and Georgia show masculine child sex ratios. But this should not be cause for comfort to us!

The new dip in the child sex ratio also signals a general policy failure and an inability to control sex determination. Can laws and palliative policies address the root causes of the malaise? The answer is no. As I have reiterated several times, it can only be the hard work of ensuring equal rights for girls and women — whether in property or in other entitlements such as education, nutrition and health care that will drive the turnaround. Parents have to value daughters — only then will they survive. Also, society has to learn to acknowledge the contributions of women and girls — and this has to be learned behaviour as the market doesn't seem to be doing it very well.

The Indian Express, Lucknow Edition, 4 April 2011.

Districts With High Literacy Show Disturbing Trend Of Low Sex Ratio, Says Ashish Tripathi

THE FLIPSIDE OF
RISING LITERACY RATE IN STATE

The increase in literacy rate in Uttar Pradesh seems to have taken a toll on the unborn girl child. And, if the 2011 Census data are to be believed, then the districts, which have made substantial gains in literacy rate have also registered a sharp decline in the child sex ratio (CSR) (0-6 age group).

Activists say that this implies that the sex determination technology and female foeticide is reaching at a faster rate to the people, as they are becoming literate.

Among other major districts in the state, which have shown an increase in literacy and decline in the CSR are Bahraich, where literacy rate went up by 16%, but, the CSR fell by 37 points. Azamgarh has registered a drop of 33 points..

Out of 71 districts in UP, nearly half have shown an increase of literacy by more than 15% in 2011 over the 2001 Census figures.

The same districts have registered a sharp fall in the CSR (number of girls per 1000 boys) of over 20 points. In Hardoi, CSR fell by 51 points, the highest in the state, whereas the literacy rate has increased by over 17% between 2001-11. Similarly, in Ballia, literacy has increased by 16% and CSR declined by 45 points in last 10 years.

Among other major districts in the state, which have shown an increase in literacy and decline in the CSR are Bahraich, where literacy rate went up by 16%, but, the CSR fell by 37 points. Azamgarh has registered a drop of 33 points in the CSR, while its literacy rate increased by 15%.

Similarly, CSR declined in Sonbhadara and Kushinagar by 36 and 38 points respectively. Here, literacy rate improved by 17% and 19% respectively.

"UP's literacy has gone up from 64.83% in 2001 to 74.04% in 2011. In the same period the CSR fell from 916 to 899. This shows that access to information about sex determination and female foeticide has become easy with the increase in literacy," said Dr Neelam Singh, member of the Central Supervisory Board formed by the Centre to implement the Pre-Conception and Pre-Natal Diagnostic Technique (prohibition of sex determination) Act 2003.

"The data also shows that more and more people irrespective of caste, income group and religion are now going for female foeticide. The backward regions of east UP and Bundelkhand have registered a good increase in literacy, but, sharp decline in CSR. Clearly, education has not brought wisdom. It seems that 'knowledge' has played evil by strengthening the patriarchal mindset," said Dr Singh.

"We need a multi-pronged strategy to counter female foeticide. Besides, strict punishment for doctors, who are involved in sex determination, people must be made aware that daughters are not burden but assets," said psychologist Manju Agarwal. Rolly Mishra, a social activist, who has studied the impact of decline in the CSR in west UP districts and Bundelkhand, said, "Low CSR has resulted in bride buying, polyandry and increase in sexual crime against woman."

Awareness campaigns for the past decade have not been able to change the mindset. "Recently, an expecting mother came to me for medical examination along with her 5-year-old daughter. The girl on seeing picture of a baby on a poster asked her mother; 'Maa is this the bhaiyya you are expecting?' Obviously, the girl must have picked it up from the conversation in the family" said Dr Singh, while exemplifying how the seeds of patriarchy are sown in a child's mind.

Dr DP Singh, a radiologist in Jaunpur, said that the need is to include the ills of sex determination in school books and motivate students to speak against female foeticide in their families and outside. Dr Sanjay Towar, a Lakhimpur-based radiologist supported the idea of including the topic in MBBS curriculum. "A young impressionable mind in first year of MBBS can be moulded in a right direction, so that they do not indulge in the evil after becoming doctors," he said.

'Ditched' by their own parents

Kshama: She was dumped by her parents in a ditch soon after the birth. But, luckily was caught amid hyacinth and later rescued by villagers, who took her to the government hospital and from there she was brought to government orphanage at Prag Narain Road. The girl suffers from physical disability. One of her leg is short. That seems to be reason why her parents chose to abandon her. The girl will steal your heart with her innocent smile.

Vaidehi: Barely few days old, this visually challenged girl was found abandoned at Ram Manohar Lohia hospital on March 15, 2010. Initially no orphanage was ready to admit her as managing disabled babies specially mentally retarded and visually challenged is very difficult. The staff in the government orphanage is not trained for it. It was only after the intervention of the child welfare committee, the girl got shelter in the government orphanage.

The Times of India, Lucknow Edition (*Times City*, Varanasi),
16 April 2011.

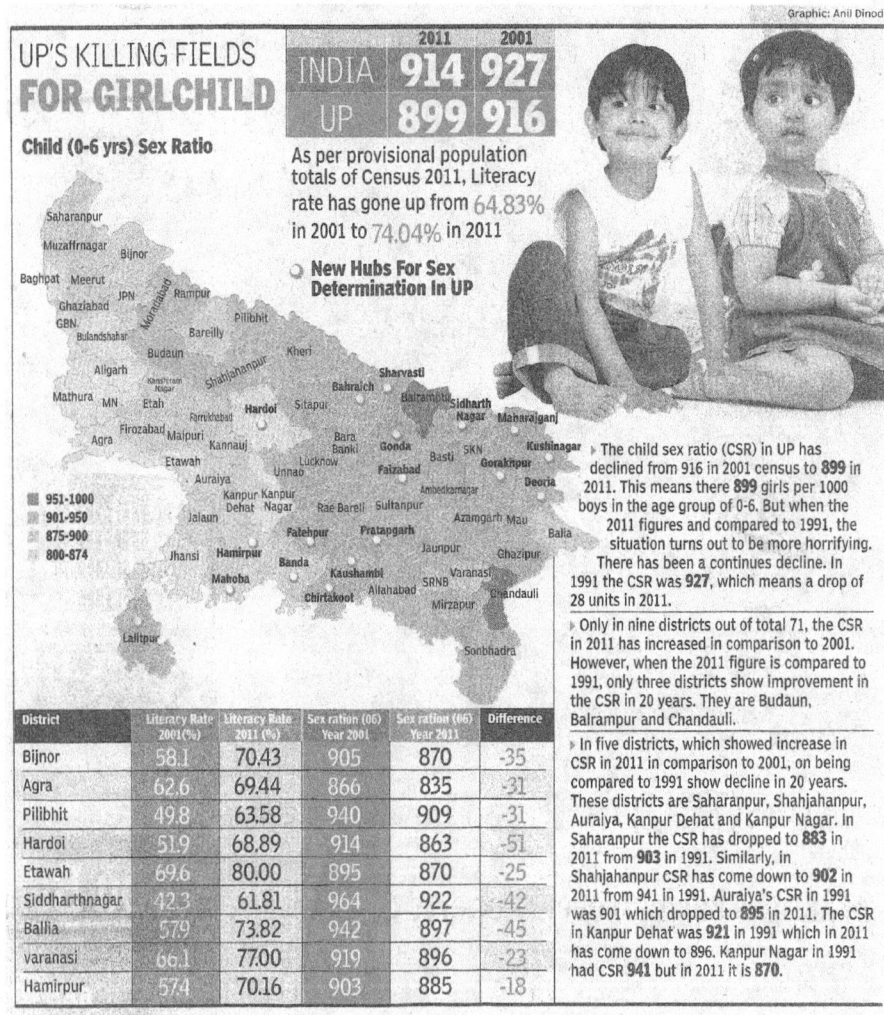

	2011	2001
INDIA	914	927
UP	899	916

UP'S KILLING FIELDS FOR GIRLCHILD

Child (0-6 yrs) Sex Ratio

As per provisional population totals of Census 2011, Literacy rate has gone up from 64.83% in 2001 to 74.04% in 2011

New Hubs For Sex Determination In UP

Graphic: Anil Dinod

- 951-1000
- 901-950
- 875-900
- 800-874

▸ The child sex ratio (CSR) in UP has declined from 916 in 2001 census to **899** in 2011. This means there **899** girls per 1000 boys in the age group of 0-6. But when the 2011 figures and compared to 1991, the situation turns out to be more horrifying. There has been a continues decline. In 1991 the CSR was **927**, which means a drop of 28 units in 2011.

▸ Only in nine districts of total 71, the CSR in 2011 has increased in comparison to 2001. However, when the 2011 figure is compared to 1991, only three districts show improvement in the CSR in 20 years. They are Budaun, Balrampur and Chandauli.

▸ In five districts, which showed increase in CSR in 2011 in comparison to 2001, on being compared to 1991 show decline in 20 years. These districts are Saharanpur, Shahjahanpur, Auraiya, Kanpur Dehat and Kanpur Nagar. In Saharanpur the CSR has dropped to **883** in 2011 from 903 in 1991. Similarly, in Shahjahanpur CSR has come down to **902** in 2011 from 941 in 1991. Auraiya's CSR in 1991 was 901 which dropped to **895** in 2011. The CSR in Kanpur Dehat was **921** in 1991 which in 2011 has come down to 896. Kanpur Nagar in 1991 had CSR **941** but in 2011 it is **870**.

District	Literary Rate 2001(%)	Literacy Rate 2011 (%)	Sex ration (06) Year 2001	Sex ration (06) Year 2011	Difference
Bijnor	58.1	70.43	905	870	-35
Agra	62.6	69.44	866	835	-31
Pilibhit	49.8	63.58	940	909	-31
Hardoi	51.9	68.89	914	863	-51
Etawah	69.6	80.00	895	870	-25
Siddharthnagar	42.3	61.81	964	922	-42
Ballia	57.9	73.82	942	897	-45
varanasi	66.1	77.00	919	896	-23
Hamirpur	57.4	70.16	903	885	-18

The Times of India, Lucknow Edition (*Times City*, Varanasi),
16 April 2011.

Abandoned to fate, girls fight social mindset

TIMES NEWS NETWORK

Lucknow: Preference for a male child has not resulted in large scale female foeticide in the state, but its ugly face has also been manifested in the form of abandoning the girl child.

On an average, 100 girls are abandoned every month in the state, while the monthly average for Lucknow is 2. Most of the girls abandoned are either disabled or those who do not fit the social definition of 'good looking'.

Social activists say that dowry and crime against woman are the two main reasons, besides patriarchal mindset that a son is must for salvation and carrying forward the family lineage.

Most of the 'good looking' girls are adopted by childless couples, but nobody adopts disabled and 'not-so-good-looking' girls. "Most of the girls abandoned are born to poor families, who consider raising a girl child as a burden," said Dharmendra, a child rights activist.

This year, so far, five girls including newborns have been found abandoned in different parts of the city, of which one died. In 2010, 22 girls were recovered from the streets. The number in 2009 was 19, while the corresponding figures for 2008 and 2007 were 17 and 16 respectively. Abandoned baby boys were also recovered. But, their number was 1% of the girls. The abandoned boys, activists feel are perhaps those born to unmarried mothers. Interestingly, boys are adopted as soon as they are admitted in the orphanages.

A couple of orphanages in the city including Manisha Mandir have put a cradle outside the premises with the request that people may leave the baby in the cradle instead of throwing them in bushes or ditches. People may also hand over the babies to the orphanage without disclosing their identity. But, still many continue to abandon the girl child on the streets.

Most of the abandoned babies are found in and outside Charbagh railway station or in and outside Alambagh bus station.

"This shows that parents come from adjoining districts, leave their babies and go back. They apparently think that somebody would get babies to the orphanages. However, those dumping babies in garbage or ditches are really heartless," said Varsha Sharma, co-ordinator, Childline.

The Times of India, Lucknow Edition (*Times City*, Varanasi), 16 April 2011.

Sex determination and female foeticide are not a small-town phenomena, but also prevalent in big districts like Lucknow, Kanpur, Allahabad and Varanasi, finds a study done by TOI

BIG CITIES,
Big Offenders

LUCKNOW

In Lucknow, the child sex ratio (CSR), that is, number of girls per thousand boys, as per census 2011, is 913, a fall of two units in comparison to 2001. The city has around 350 ultrasound and diagnostic centres. In-vitro fertilisation facilities are also available which can produce son or daughter as per the choice of the parents.

A survey done by students of Ram Mahonar Lohia University with the help of Vatsalya showed that nearly 75 centres in the city were covertly offering sex determination facility.

Mainly situated in Indiranagar, Chowk and Aliganj, Sarojininagar and Sitapur road, the centres were admitted that they do sex determination when students approached them as a client. Students also tried to shoot the conversation with their mobile phones but at most places they were asked to deposit their phone sets at the reception.

"While 15 centres readily accepted to do the service, others said that they would decide after seeing the woman. The price was between Rs 1,600 to Rs 2,500. Only one centre refused," said Anjani Kumar, social activist, who supervised the survey.

"A few centres were sealed after a surprise inspection by a team of officials of government of India and state health officers two years back for not following the norms. Some have not applied for renewal but are said to be using machines as mobile units or for back door facilities," he said.

VARANASI

In Varanasi, CSR is down from 919 in 2001 to 896 in 2011, a drop by 23 units. Dr RS Verma, the chief medical officer, told TOI that there were about 150 registered ultrasound clinics in the district. He also claimed that there was no unauthorised ultrasound centre in the district and that he has no information of any case of female foeticide. He said that the health department conducts drives time to time to check the validity of ultrasound centres.

"We have conducted about 15 surprise raids to keep tab on operation of ultrasound centres in the district in the last one month," said Dr AN Singh, additional chief medical officer.

He said that notices had been served on as many as 14 ultrasound centres asking them to come up with proper and valid documents. However, a survey conducted by a local NGO Vishal Bharat Sansthan (VBS) contradicts claims of health officials. According to Rajiv Srivastava of VBS, there are over 150 registered and many unregistered ultrasound centres in Varanasi. About 150 families from different districts of eastern UP and Bihar come to Varanasi everyday for sex determination of children, he said, adding that despite the ban on sex determination, the practice continued in the district.

The NGO's point seems to be valid with the fact that perhaps for the first time an FIR of female foeticide was lodged on the direction of the district magistrate on June 16 2009.

A woman, Reena, resident of Tendui village met the district magistrate (DM) alleging that her husband Jitendra Vishwakarma, who is a compounder, killed her female foetus after sex determination. On the instruction of the DM the case was registered with Jansa police.

The Sunday Times of India, Lucknow Edition, 17 April 2011.

Sex determination and female foeticide are not a small-town phenomena, but also prevalent in big districts like Lucknow, Kanpur, Allahabad and Varanasi, finds a study done by TOI

BIG CITIES, Big Offenders

KANPUR

The CSR has increased in Kanpur by one unit in 2011 in comparison to 2001. It was 869 in 2001 and now 870 but when compared to 941 CSR in 1991, the fall in 20 years is of 71 units. The city has over 250 registered ultrasound centres. The Kanpur district administration had launched a drive against the genetic counselling centres violating the provision of PCPNDT Act.

As many as 67 out of 192 city based ultrasound centres were served show cause notice in March 2010. Out of the 29 centres that did not responded to the notice and failed to explain their stand lost their license on April 21, on the orders of former district magistrate, Amrit Abhijaat.

Around 17 ultrasound machines were sealed due to anamolies in 'Form F'- a form to specify the purpose behind ultrasound done during pregnancy. The district administration has sufficient evidences to register cases against the ultrasound centre but no legal action has been initiated even after an year.

Legal adviser of the District Advisory Committee, formed under PCPNDT Act, Manish Kumar Sharma, said that the reports were submitted few months ago but no action has been taken by the officials.

ALLAHABAD

In Allahabad, the CSR has come down from 917 in 2001 to 902 in 2011. Social activists say that there are over 60 ultrasound centres in and around the district. "The sex determination was rampant here but authorities have been strict for the past some years, as a result of which, the problem has been controlled in the city up to some extent but it persists in outskirts like Naini, Jhusi and Fafamau," said Anil Singh Bhadauria, social activist and teacher in Rajshree Tandon Open University.

He said that till five years back, there used to be no registration of even nursing homes. Naseem Ansari, a social activist, said that though situation has improve in the Allahabad city, the centres in

Backward districts more prone?

Sex determination and female foeticide have also gripped backward districts with high below poverty line population. Take example of Hardoi which has witnessed a drop in CSR from 914 to 863 (51 units) in past ten years. The population living below poverty line in Hardoi is 74%, ie one third of the total people in the district. Similarly, in Ballia over half of the population is below poverty line and CSR 2011 is 897, down 45 units in comparison to 942 in 2001. Siddharthnagar has witnessed a decline of 42 units in the CSR in past ten years.

The district has over 42% population living below poverty line. In Kushinagar, 42% population comes under below poverty line and the decline in CSR in 2011 is 38 units in comparison to 2001. Sonbhadra has over 80% population below poverty line and the district has witnessed a decline of CSR by 36 units.

Experts say that earlier the practice of sex determination and female foeticide was prevalent in middle and upper middle class due to patriarchal mindset and social insecurity associated with girl child. But, now technology has reached backward areas. Apart from other reasons, poor families go for costly sex determination test and female foeticide as raising a girl child is comparatively expensive, they said.

the outskirts are catering to neighbouring districts like Pratapgarh, Kaushambi and Chitrakoot. "Awareness campaigns and regular monitoring of registered ultrasound clinics has brought the desired results," said additional Director (Health) Dr Asha Bhargava.

Inputs from Ashish Tripathi, Binay Singh, Faiz Rehman Siddiqui and Kapil Dixit

The Sunday Times of India, Lucknow Edition, 17 April 2011.

Reference

Filmography

Amar, Mehboob Khan, 1954.

Ankur, Shyam Benegal, 1973.

Nishant, Shyam Benegal, 1978.

Matrubhoomi: *A Nation without Women*, Manish Jha, 2003.

Fiction

Anand, Mulk Raj. *Gauri* (*The Old Woman and the Cow*). New Delhi: Arnold-Heinemann, 1981 (1960).

Perspectives on Gender

Uma, A. *Woman and her family*. New Delhi: Sterling, 1989.

Mukherjee, Geetanjali (Ed.). *Dowry Death in India*. Delhi: Indian Publishers Distributors, 1999.

Manier, Bénédicte. *Quand les femmes auront disparu. L'élimination des filles en Inde et en Asie*. Paris: La Découverte, 2006.

Patel, Tulsi (Ed.). *Sex-selective Abortion in India, Gender, Society and New Reproductive Technologies*. New Delhi: Sage, 2007.

Sharada, Srinivasan. *Daughter Deficit. Sex Selection in Tamil Nadu*. New Delhi: Women Unlimited, 2011.

Newspapers

"Trend of Female Foeticide Catching Up Very Fast", in *The Hindu*, Lucknow Edition, 31 January 2011.

Kounteya Sinha, "In 20 Yrs, 20% More Men than Women", in *The Times of India*, Lucknow Edition, 17 March 2011.

Smita Kumar, "Women in State Make Sense of Census", in *The Telegraph*, Calcutta (Bihar, Patna Edition), 2 April 2011.

Ravinder Kaur, "The Index of Inequality", in *The Indian Express*, Lucknow Edition, 4 April 2011.

Vimal Bhatia, "Infanticide in this Village of 13 Girls?", in *The Times of India*, Lucknow Edition, 5 April 2011.

"The Day is Not Far ...", in *The Times of India*, Lucknow Edition, 13 April 2011.

"The Flipside of Rising Literacy Rate in State", "Abandoned to Fate, Girls Fight Social Mindset", in *The Times of India*, Lucknow Edition (*Times City*, Varanasi), 16 April 2011.

"Big Cities, Big Offenders", in *The Sunday Times of India*, Lucknow Edition, 17 April 2011.

Dancing Marriage Away and Back in *Rab Ne Bana Di Jodi.*

Carole Rozzonelli

In Indian marriage continuity and discontinuity interlap each other quite closely. As far as the bride is concerned, she leaves her father's house and assumes a new identity, that is, a fixed and pre-established role and the household duties that follow. This implies a sharp initial possible distinction between individual love and depersonalised behaviour. The marriage between Surinder (Suri) and Taani (Tanu) in *Rab Ne Bana Di Jodi* (*A Couple Made in Heaven*, 2008) answers at first this fragmenting condition, one here of partial estrangement. She tells him that they are going to be a pro-forma couple and that she won't change at all her mindset and her previous ways of life. Thus their conjugality does not share emotions or personal feelings, but turns around the observance on her part of a minimum of household responsibilities. In particular, she cooks for him excellent food, which will be also hugely appreciated by his colleagues. She never trespasses on the passive respect of *rekha* [the forbidding line for women] – when the intruding colleagues of her husband self-invite themselves to a dinner party. The otherwise absentee wife meets at last her guests, to uphold her husband's honour. She accepts for a while her domestic role of provider of food for them – as a matter of fact the *khana-daana* (the gift of food) is a basic duty in feminine conjugal and social life as a hostess. The problem lies in the fact that her husband has romantically and deeply fallen in love as soon as he first saw her – so he accepts, at least in a temporary way, this one-way relationship.

Romance introduces a dynamic urge and enthusiasm within an otherwise bleak conjugal life – as a matter of fact they marry after the fatal accident which has killed her perspective groom and his whole family. Suri takes care of Tanu, who accepts the marriage with him just to please her worrying father. Different types of duty (or dharmic responsibilities) are at work here: the professor-student relationship (one moulded on tradition), the obedience a daughter must give to her father, the responsibility a husband has for his wife, the role a married woman has in the making up of a family. These notions of duty loom large in the conceptual background of the film, especially if one considers how the Manu body of laws recognises no autonomy in life to a woman – she always ought to be under the guardianship or the patronage of a man, either her father, a brother or her husband.[1]

Although a marriage of responsibility, the union between Suri and Tanu transcends the practice of the arranged marriage – it should rather be interpreted from a mere ideological point of view, whose stern abstractness is progressively and finally corrected by romance on the part of the man. He reacts to obstructed or impeded love and subsequent estrangement in everyday life. He creates discontinuity in his life, as an individual surrogate to the emotional side which his marriage is deprived of. As a matter of fact the trick he employs of an assumed identity is grounded again on a basic notion that in a Hindu marriage love should be the consequence of marriage and not the other way around. So, his behaviour does not imply at all a strategy of change in married life, but just resorts to an astute trick to achieve a legitimate end; love after tying the knot.

He pays lip service to modernity by inscribing his wife, (and successively himself) to a Bombayite course of dance, and by assuming a cinematic fake identity. Thus Suri introduces a film within the film, that is, a metarepresentation of an imagined role which dramatises the acting persona and leads to possible splitting confusion in marriage. Now arises an apparently schizoid mood, one which domesticates safely the enigma of individuality traced quite dramatically in *Raat Aur Din* (*Darkness and Light*, 1967). To avoid the trap of schizophrenia *Rab Ne Bana Di Jodi* uses the time-honoured expedient of the disguised self: metaphorically the character enters a door as himself and goes out as the other.

This exchange of identities within the same person, from introvert and timid to extrovert and vice versa, has been dealt with in *Jeans* (1998), a cybernetic comedy in which the bedtrick is paramount to the

[1] Doniger, Wendy, and Brian K. Smith (Eds.). *Le Leggi di Manu*. Milano: Adelphi, 1996 (1991), Chapter V, pp. 147-151.

intricacies of the practices concerning the arranged marriage and the poison tree which the Indian family can sometimes be. *Rab Ne Bana Di Jodi* exploits only in parts the time-honoured mechanism of the frenzied bedtrick. As a matter of fact it also refers to the drama or melodrama of the dutiful marriage, such as featured in the tormented love stories of the Seventies: *Dil Ek Mandir* (*The Heart, a Temple*, 1963), for instance. With a seminal difference however, since *Rab Ne Bana Di Jodi* shifts the emphasis from melodrama to domestic comedy.

Differently from the pristine cinematic heroines, Tanu can forget herself and her drab domestic life by dancing away her virtual marriage. All passion seems to be spent with her, whose only aim left in life seems to be the prize in the course final competition. Her mimicking husband is instructed by her to proficient partnership in dance, notwithstanding and beyond his unredeemable clumsiness. Of course his assumed identity is just an exterior veneer which does not even scratch his own true nature. Considering this perspective the film evades almost totally whatever doubt or tension concerning a possible double identity within the same person – instead of duality one should speak of a parodic rendering of assertive virility. The man in the dancing couple is undoubtedly Tanu, as shown by the semi-farcical episode of the quarrel with another couple.

So, Raj Kapoor (the alter ego of Suri) and Tanu do not actually form a team, even if she seems for a while on the verge of falling in love with him. Once again *Rab Ne Bana Di Jodi* falls back on the stereotype of fidelity in marriage and eventually on self-sacrifice, this time on the part of the husband. However, the true kernel of the film deals with the taming to domesticity of an absentee wife, according to the sophistication of a very common assessment in Hindu matrimonial ethos: love is after marriage and not vice versa. In any case, before reaching its climax the film (we should not forget the namesake adopted by Suri, that is, Raj Kapoor) borders a bit dangerously on the "three is a crowd" syndrome which leads to tragedy in *Sangam* (*Confluence*, 1964). This concealed quotation might perhaps indicate an inside joke within the plot of the film, with a clever metaphor of substitution or at least of double presence and consequent rivalry (Suri against Raj Kapoor).

However, Raj Kapoor is just a shadow of the real being, and as such is doomed to vanish into Suri as soon his (or its) task has been duly accomplished. In the ending of the film it is Suri who dances triumphally his wife to victory. The real metamorphosis of identity in *Rab Ne Bana Di Jodi* concerns as a matter of fact the submission of the married woman. This is the real trick within the plot. On the other side the unrealistic doubling of Suri starts a metafilm. In fact Suri behaves like a typical Shah Rukh Khan character (one should not forget the incipit in the railway station of *Dil Se..*, *The Ways of the Heart*, 1998), with more than a hint of standard comedy and technological modernisation. The unrealistic doubling of the characters reaches as far back as the "comedy of the errors" archetype, one often involving two twins, opposite in characters and manners. A model available for the film might be found in *Jeans* (1998), in which an invented twin sister represents a possible other side of the modernising heroine. The exchange of identities happens the other way around in *Rab Ne Bana Di Jodi*, from introversion to extroversion, at least on the surface.

The computer-created image which in *Jeans* determines, rather catastrophically in the ending, the metaphors of control concerning the duplicity of the persona is replaced in *Rab Ne Bana Di Jodi* with the blindness concerning love shown by Tanu. She is not interested at all in her conjugal life, actually a no-life she accepts just out of practical reasons. Her heart and passions are exclusively devoted to dancing. So she cannot recognise her husband, a virtual character without concrete existence for her. To be acknowledged, Suri has to enter her imagined world and he (or it?) comes true to her eyes by assuming a filmi identity. To a literary-minded audience this is but a flimsy escamotage, a mere cinematic trick which actually changes the one who is unreal into a real being.

So, the agency of cinematic mimicry allows visibility to one who is invisible – the namesake Raj Kapoor is the key to love in marriage, but Suri's real identity also represents, notwithstanding his apparent bureaucratic grey nature, a figure of provincial male bourgeois whose behaviour is not aggressive, as in the Bachchan type, but reflexive and utterly representative of an *aam* (common man) Indian identity, even in his transition through marriage from *mussafil* (provincial) to crypto-urbanite. To conquer the love of her wife he has to merge within himself the two types of the virile hero rather on the maverick side and of the average modern *babu* (clerk). However, the performative space of action opened by this double role is still ruled by the structural clumsiness traditionally attributed, at least in the colonial ages, to *babus*. Eventually it is a third persona who saves the day – that is, the husband, the self-sacrificing invisible man, the domestic hero whose previous liminality moves once for all to the centre stage. He reifies the ethos of marriage through a crossover transition from an obstructed domesticity to an achieved position as a full recognised husband.

From a complementary perspective, Tanu embodies modernity and consumerism, whereas Suri stands for a more cultured status. Marriage (that is, the observance of duties) is the intermediate space which regulates the meeting of differences. The division is clear cut since the beginning – Suri is the bread winner (Tanu does not have any financial autonomy) and the wife cooks and cleans the house. The crossover between tradition and modernity opens a space of moderate liberal ideology within the frame of the film – cosmopolitan Mumbai compromises with the *mussafil* style of life and vice versa, in a plea for a maintained identity through accommodating behaviours.

Filmography

Dil Ek Mandir, C.V. Shridhar, 1963.

Sangam, Raj Kapoor, 1964.

Raat Aur Din, Satyen Bose, 1967.

Dil Se.. , Mani Ratnam, 1998.

Jeans, S. Shankar, 1998.

Rab Ne Bana Di Jodi, Aditya Chopra, 2008.

Bollywood Framing Kashmir Valley: Violence and Victims.

Neha Pandey

The state of *Jammu and Kashmir* has a strategic importance for India, both politically and emotionally. *Kashmir* is synonymous with heaven, valley, conflict-zone and an insolvable issue. It has different meanings for different people at different times and such stratification is mutually exclusive. India and Pakistan have been disputing ownership over the Kashmir region for many years, this resulting in high levels of exposure to violence among the civilian population. For some what is termed freedom struggle is actually a sense of misery, deprivation, shock and captivity for million others. In any crisis situation, victims lose their hopes, identities, their significance and sense of pride. The weaker and the most vulnerable sections of society like the aged, the women and the children are the worst affected. Also, for any religion or ideology, the faith and dignity of our men folk rest with the purity and sacrosanctity of their women. When this faith and belief is tarnished or attacked, the rage and atrocities multiply and grow sporadically.

Cinema maestro Ritwik Ghatak has mentioned, "Any story is good material if it contains the scope for those nuances. Even the songs and dances are not loads around your neck. They are creative elements with tremendous potentials, if the theme and approach calls for them".[1] The Mumbai-located film industry of India, Bollywood, has accorded a place of pride and concern to this sensitive issue of dealing with Kashmir and its multi-faceted problems. This article is an attempt to describe which issues (Kashmir-related) have been highlighted by the Indian-Bollywood directors and the plight of women and children as depicted in those films over the last two decades. An elaborate analysis

---

[1] Ghatak, Ritwik. *Cinema and I*. Calcutta: Ritwik Memorial Trust, 1987, p. 17.

has been done of these films – *Roja* (1992), *Dil Se..* (*The Ways of the Heart*, 1998), *Mission Kashmir* (2000) and *Lamhaa* (*Moment*, 2010).

Time-Framing the Events

The two decades from 1990 to 2010 have been selected because it was 1989 when insurgency was at its peak in Kashmir valley and its repercussions have an echo today as well. An attempt has been made to study the turn of events and their glimpses in the Bollywood reel.

Method: First, a brief introduction of the plot has been given followed by criteria-specific analysis. Later a comparative and descriptive approach has been adopted. Other elements which have been incorporated in this chapter for better understanding of the issues are: Political situation, Religion, Reason, Perspective, Women, Children, Victim, Justification, Song/Dance, Word Usage, Box-Office success and Accolade. They are either discussed separately or in a combined form.

Significance of Song and Dance: Many have raised eyebrows as to why Indian cinema-makers have given so much of reel-space to song and dance. Any art or media mirrors back a specific culture. Same is the case with Bollywood's fantasy and engrossment with song and dance. It has been part and parcel of Indian tradition, culture, identity and integrity for ages. This is a genuine justification to the fact that song and dance occupy and will continue to occupy this place on reels and space in our mental frame. A sense of belongingness comes from there. Also it provides a vent for our emotional troubles and problems and is synonymous with the cathartic effect of drama.

According to Ritwik Ghatak, "Film is not a form, it has forms. Nobody denies the special privileges of cine-camera, but one should not approach the issue from that side at all – one should approach it from the point of view of the emotions aroused and intellects sharpened by one's end product: the result that accrues, after all, you create 'for' the people. I believe in committed cinema".[2] A film captures the complex texture of time, subtle humanity, shades of relationships, song of despair and colour tones which play emotional roles in cinema.

---

[2] Ghatak, Ritwik, *op.cit.*, p. 15.

The Issue of Kashmir – Background

Militancy in the disputed region of Kashmir has been a major fuel for discord between India and Pakistan since the 1980s. Attacks in the region began to increase in scale and intensity following the Soviet invasion of Afghanistan. The foreign insurgents flooded the region to join the Afghan Mujahideen to fight against the Soviet forces. India now holds about two-thirds of the territory of Kashmir, which it calls Jammu and Kashmir. Pakistan controls about one-third, which it calls *Azad* (meaning 'free') Kashmir. China also controls two small sections of northern Kashmir.

The U.S. State Department lists three Islamist groups active in Kashmir as foreign terrorist organisations: Harakat ul-Mujahideen, Jaish-e-Mohammed, and Lashkar-e-Taiba.[3] An outfit calling itself the Indian Mujahideen came to light in 2008 with multiple large scale terror attacks. On November 26, 2008, a group calling itself the Deccan Mujahideen claimed responsibility for a string of attacks across Mumbai.[4]

The Soviet Invasion of Afghanistan

In Christmas 1979, Russian paratroopers landed in Kabul, the capital of Afghanistan. The Prime Minister, Hazifullah Amin, tried to sweep aside Muslim tradition within the nation and wanted a more western slant to Afghanistan. This outraged the majority of the Afghans, as a strong tradition of Muslim belief was common in the country.

Thousands of Afghanistan Muslims joined the Mujahideen - a guerilla force on a holy mission for Allah. They wanted to overthrow the Amin government. This was also extended to the Russians who were now in Afghanistan trying to maintain the power of the Amin government. The Russians claimed that their task was to support a legitimate government and that the Mujahideen were no more than terrorists.

By the end of the 1980s, the Mujahideen were at war in Afghanistan, with hard line Taliban fighters taking a stronger grip over

---

[3] [http://www.cfr.org/kashmir/kashmir-militant-extremists/p9135, accessed 18 September 2011].

[4] [http://en.wikipedia.org/wiki/Mujahideen, accessed 18 September 2011].

the whole nation and imposing very strict Muslim law on the Afghanistan population.[5] In 1989, the Soviet soldiers were withdrawn by Moscow. The Mujahideen and its various outfits, aided by the Inter-Services Intelligence Agency of Pakistan, then looked at Kashmir as the Taliban rule swept through Afghanistan. This situation has prompted the increased terrorists' activities in Kashmir.

Roja (1992) – A Film by Mani Ratnam

The first scene opens in Kashmir, where a dangerous terrorist, Wasim Khan, is arrested by a team led by Colonel Rayappa (Nassar). In South India, Roja (played by Madhoo) is a simple village girl born and brought up in Southern Tamil Nadu. Roja is married to Rishi Kumar (played by Arvind Swamy), a top cryptologist working with the Indian government. The couple moves to Madras (present day Chennai). Meanwhile, Rishi is assigned a posting to an army communications center in Kashmir. Roja's world turns upside down when Rishi is abducted by the terrorists whose agenda is to separate Kashmir from India and to free their leader, Wasim Khan, from judicial custody. Faced with the daunting task of rescuing her husband, Roja runs from pillar to post, pleading with politicians and the military for help. Further complicating matters is the communication gap as she cannot speak their language, and they cannot speak hers.

Meanwhile Rishi, held captive by a group of terrorists led by Liaqat (played by Pankaj Kapur), tries to reason with them. The government decides to release Wasim Khan in exchange for the release of Rishi. Rishi, not wanting to be used as a pawn to release a dangerous terrorist, gets help from the sympathetic Liaqat's sister and escapes. Liaqat catches up with him and holds him at gun point. Rishi reasons with Liaqat further and convinces her that his war is immoral.[6]

Political Situation: Armed resistance to Indian rule broke out in the Kashmir valley in 1989, with some groups calling for independence and others calling for union with Pakistan. India accused Pakistan of supplying the militants with weapons. During the 1990s, with the emergence of militant Muslim groups, the movement's ideology shifted from a nationalistic and secularist one to an Islamic one.

---

[5] [http://www.guidetorussia.com/russia-afghanistan.asp, accessed 13 September 2011].
[6] [http://encyclopedia.xoila.com/?title=Roja, accessed 17 August 2011].

Religion: The protagonist is a Hindu while the leader of the separatist group is a Muslim who is shown offering Namaaz. When he is questioned by the protagonist if Islam allows the killing of one man by another, he has no words or is not aware of the guiltiness implied in his stand.

Reason: The separatist leader believes in *jihad* which calls for the separation of Kashmir from Indian rule. This is established by his own understanding and reasoning in one of the scenes where Rishi asks him about his motive. Rishi tries to reason out that Pakistan is fuelling this agenda by providing weapons and training. However, this belief in Pakistan on the part of the separatist is finally shaken when innocent and young boys, including his younger brother, belonging to his group on their way to Pakistan for training are gunned down by a patrol of the Pakistani Army.

Perspective: The matter needs to be resolved through talks and violence will never reap any solution. This is what the protagonist maintains. India will never give Kashmir away, as it is an integral part of its territory. Indian soldiers are shown in positive framework, given how they sacrifice anything and everything to keep Indians safe and secure. Even the minister's character is shown as one who is very supportive and concerning.

Women: The story revolves around the protagonist's wife, Roja, a religious Hindu devout who fights with administration, police, army, minister and even the terrorist Wasim Khan in order to get her husband back. She knows that the release of a hard-core separatist and killer is no way justifiable. The question of nation versus wife unsettles her and she progressively yields to the demand for the liberation of her husband. There is another strong female character in the movie. The silent Muslim girl has a soft corner for Rishi and helps him fleeing. She is the sister of the separatist leader and offers Rishi food and advice. This clearly gives a positive message of sense of brotherhood and compassion between ordinary Hindus and Muslims.

Victim: However, the film does not bring the audience anywhere near to the real plight of the Kashmiris directly. There is curfew everywhere and a deafening silence in the valley except for gun shots which run across the length and breadth of the movie. Because of that many have left the valley or are captivated in their home. There is a scene where Roja offers a coconut to a Hindu deity, and the sound of breaking the coconut brings the soldiers to the venue from everywhere. This depicts that any sound in the valley has been synonymous with the sound of a bomb blast and calls for the attention and alertness of the security officials. The real victim such as portrayed in this movie is an outsider, a South Indian couple who get involved in this atmosphere of suspicion and fright. The language problem is shown effectively in a scene when Roja tries to lodge a complaint regarding the abduction of her husband.

Justification: The point of view of the director is firmly established, i.e. separatists have been misguided. They are good people and forgiving. The message – no one is a born terrorist is brought home into unsophisticated minds.

Song/Dance: The background music and songs amalgamate well with the theme and are rich in fostering a sense of pride for India, its unity and integration. There is a scene where the angered terrorists burn an Indian flag, but Rishi risks his own life to put out the fire and shows the terrorists how much the country means to him. The song *Bharat humko jaan se pyara hai* (India is dearer than life) creates an elevated mood of patriotism and love for the nation. Lyrics capture the mood of the film, which is patriotism and is far above anything and everything.

Use of Words: In the movie, the separatists are addressed as 'hard-core terrorists' by the news channels and 'puppets in the hands of Pakistan' by the protagonist.

Box-Office Success and Accolade: The film was a huge hit as a sense of patriotism ignites and unites people. Also the film received national awards beside other cine-awards. The founding event in the film (Rishi's abduction) found its counterpart in reality. Rubiya Sayeed, the daughter of the Indian Home Minister, was kidnapped on 8 December 1989. She was released a few days later in exchange for five militants held in an Indian jail.[7]

---

[7] [http://news.bbc.co.uk/2/hi/south_asia/8400176.stm, accessed 29 September 2011].

Dil Se.. (1998) – A Film by Mani Ratnam

Another movie which captures the distress, agony, anger and wrath of the Kashmiris is *Dil Se*. It is a film made to coincide with the fifty years of India's Independence Day celebrations. The story is focused on the member of a separatist organisation, a suicide bomber (Meghna played by Manisha Koirala), who is trained to kill the president as part of the agenda. She is a female rebel who questions her admirer, *'darr kise kehte hain iska ehsaas bhi hai tumhe?'* (Can you ever feel what terror is?). In the film, it has been firmly established that the rebel (Meghna) has been victimised and vandalised as a result of the Kashmir conflict. Later, it is revealed that when she was 12 years old her village was burnt, her family killed and she was raped. She has lost her identity and existence since that harrowing incident. That episode has left deep psychological shocks and scars. She is unable to speak when she relives these memories. Thus, the film captures the psychological trauma of a child victimised by terrorism and communal violence and depicts the same feeling for the audience.

It deeply reflects the mental frame of victimised and traumatised children. The next scene captures the girl along with other such children taking oath under a supervisor to gain freedom and to sacrifice body, life and soul for the complete independence of Kashmir. She has many questions in her eyes and she justifies her act by saying, "if the Indian government can't give us justice, can't we ask for it?" This is not just a question but the defining principle of all militants.

Then there are the shaken up moments when she tries to overcome all this and tries to live a normal life. She talks about her mother, her love, her would-be family and children. She bursts into tears when one member of her group is killed. But every time she tries to become humane, she is forcibly reminded of her mission by her group members and this ends all her dreams and hopes to lead a normal life. She is followed everywhere and there is no privacy in her life.

She has learnt how to constrain her basic emotions and focused energy. She knows that her life will end at any moment and so she never commits to Amar (played by Shah Rukh Khan) who is madly in love with her. She has a soft spot for him but that remains buried in one corner of her heart. She does not want him to get involved in all this.

She questions, "In order to take revenge from few culprits, why are we killing innocent people?".

Special Role of Songs: All the songs are in dream sequence, this signifying how the characters would wish to live but are not allowed to do, given circumstances in real life. Songs become a vent for those feelings and emotions. They act as a hyperventilating medium. The film features five songs, which engage in a combination of strategies and diegeses. The use of fantasy diegeses and their formalisations by the cinematic apparatus, as swift cuts and multiple angle shots, works to heighten the hyper-reality of songs and dances as well as its detachment and then by hyper-reality reconciliation with the story proper. These songs bifurcate the text and reveal the boundary between dream and reality.[8]

Two Parallels: Through the use of two female characterisations, the director has drawn two parallels in the movie. One is a victim turned militant (played by Manisha Koirala) in the form of a human bomb; the other is a simple girl (played by Preity Zinta) who wants to marry and settle down. Born in the same country, they both have experienced entirely different lives. Their agendas are strikingly different which drives home the point that the agendas of human beings are shaped by socio-cultural circumstances. Again there is another parallel. A group of school children singing "saare jahan se achha Hindustan humara" (of all the places in this world, our country is the best) for Independence Day celebrations, and another group of children taking the pledge of complete independence.

This film failed to vow audience in general but got critique awards. Indian psychology is such that it likes to see tragedy but accepts it only if it ends on a positive note. The film was a difficult one for the audience (beyond their perception and acceptance), as they could not imagine their hero and his beloved to die on the silver screen in the last scene, as was the case with *Dil Se*. Thus, the film does not end well and the film ending did not click right with the audience. The songs became more popular than the film itself.

---

[8] Gehlawat, Ajay. "The Bollywood Song and Dance, or Making a Culinary Theatre from Dung-Cakes and Dust.", in *Reframing Bollywood: Theories of Popular Hindi Cinema*. New Delhi: Sage, 2010, pp. 30-52.

Mission Kashmir (2000) – A Film by Vidhu Vinod Chopra

The film's opening says that it is dedicated to *Kashmiriyat* – the centuries old tradition of religious tolerance and harmony. Then it addresses a great deal of issues in bits and pieces. The separatists here again are labelled as terrorists and Indian police officials as the guardians and saviors of the Kashmir valley.

The most beautiful part of the film is its canvas which captures the hills, the snows, the trees, the lakes, the flowers, the culture, and the beauty of Kashmir. It presents a thoughtful contrast to the whole communal violence debate. The film speaks strongly about the religious sentiments of both Hindus and Muslims; these feelings are their biggest strength as well as their biggest weakness. It presents the traumatised agony of the Kashmiri pundits who were forcibly driven out of their land, and also evokes indirectly the plight of the Sikhs who bore the brunt of the communal riots of 1984, when the then Indian Prime Minister Indira Gandhi was assassinated by her own Sikh security guards.

> The persecution by Muslim extremists of the Hindu minority and the systematic religion-based extremism of terrorist elements has resulted in the exodus of 250,000 members of the Hindu and other minorities from the Kashmir Valley to other parts of India. Militants in Jammu and Kashmir continue to use kidnappings to sow terror, seek the release of detained comrades, and extort funds.[9]

The story is centered on the Kashmiri boy Altaaf, whose family gets killed by DIG [Deputy Inspector General] Khan who mistakes them for accomplices of the terrorists, since they give shelter to them. The same terrorist group has issued a fatwa to the purpose that doctors should not provide service to any police official in the region. Because of this fatwa, Khan loses his only son who succumbs to his injuries as the doctor refuses to treat him. His psychological wound justifies his physical act of cruelty in which an innocent family is shot down, including their six-year old daughter.

---

[9] [http://www.globalsecurity.org/military/world/war/kashmir.htm, accessed 21 October 2011].

For Altaaf, it is a loss of family, shelter, solace, future and childhood. He is adopted by the bereaved DIG Khan. His sufferings grow and his frustrations show up in his drawings. He draws sketches of the masked man and desires to kill him. When he discovers that the man who has adopted him (DIG Khan) was the perpetrator of the slaughter, he unsuccessfully shoots him and escapes in the dark. His flight signifies the world of darkness, the world of terrorism where he is heading. His only mission in life is to kill the murderer of his family and he is beguiled by the terrorist/separatist Hilal who uses him later to give shape to Mission Kashmir. Mission Kashmir, as envisaged by Hilal and the other separatists, wants to snatch Kashmir away from India, with a vision that gradually all the Muslims from India (who outnumber those who are in Pakistan) would join the independent land and will foster *jihad* as a shining star in the whole Mujahideen world. The whole contract to accomplish this mission is fixed at two crore dollars. This indicates the blanket of business which is linked to and feeding terrorism.

The black memories from Altaaf's childhood are so haunting that he is unable to sleep and sense the beauty of the valley. This brings one to the core of another important issue. It is very difficult for a child to witness and live with a trauma concerning the killing of his family. The whole life gets topsy-turvy. It is true for all such victims, especially children. Few have the courage to live with it. Some take the wrong side and get attached to a terrorist organisation in order to give shape and pace to their personal revenge motif.

The film has two strong female characters who are brave, intelligent, and adaptive to the situation. One is Altaaf's adopter, Neelima, who notwithstanding losing her only child still gathers the strength to give her husband and Altaaf a ray of hope in accepting reality. She persuades Altaaf not to destroy Kashmir. She is caught in the dichotomy of father-son relationship. On the other hand, there is the young and vivacious Sufi who is a smart journalist. She gives priority to her nation and land rather than to her newly-found love for her childhood friend Altaaf. She leaves him and blames him for committing such insane activities.

Songs are heavily packed with patriotism and love for the land. It speaks about the current tension and the agony of the blood-bathed

Kashmir-valley. It captures the local terrain, dance, music styles and costumes. This is a movie about patriotism, love, hatred, marriage, adoption, revenge, duty, religion, identity, emotion, reconciliation, pride, chance and circumstances. The frame of reference shifts from character to character. The story unfolds from each character's personal point of view giving voice to diverse opinions and not typecasting just a few. It captures not only actions but holds mirror to their minds, internal conflicts, tensions and thoughts. It is a psychoanalytic film which anatomises the pandemic of terrorism and violence that has engulfed Kashmir and the whole of India. The film has many messages and points of views. The film was a big hit in India.

Lamhaa – The Untold Story of Kashmir (2010) – A Film by Rahul Dholakia

This film reveals a complex and mysterious nexus of intelligence officials, politicians, militants, the army, all of them involved in the business of generating money from the corporate entity called Kashmir.

Uniqueness: This plot gives a totally different perspective of the issue. All the previous films have focused on victims, the separatists/militants and the military. *Lamhaa*, although including these groups, unveils a new face within them. It reveals that their ultimate agenda is nowhere near independence but towards monetary gains and profits which are generated in the business concerning the Kashmir issue. That is why there is no deliberate attempt to resolve this otherwise profitable business called Kashmir. Another point clearly depicts that whoever is agreeable with the current state of affairs in the conflict zone has the backing and support of the Indian government in forming his own rule in the state. Such a bold attempt has never been made before by any director making films on Kashmir.

The film revolves around the 1989 issue and the situation two decades afterwards. Kashmiri pundits were forced to flee from their homeland. The movie gives one very strong message: terrorism has no colour and religion. The victims have been Hindus at the hands of militants and Muslims at the hands of the army. But the fact remains unaltered that are the Kashmiris who bore and are continuously bearing the brunt. For them curfew is the order of the day and normalcy the biggest abnormality. In one scene, a driver builds up his courage and speaks his mind, "it's better to die once than to survive in this everyday-death like scenario". This sentence brings out the anguish and helplessness of the people. Then there are women in a village who still ignore after two decades if their husbands are dead or alive. Every time one of them questions the system, "at least accord me the status of widow. I can tolerate that. Tell me the truth", she is silenced.

The female protagonist boasts that every Kashmiri has got anger in *virasat* (legacy). Not only this, she happens to locate a market in which again everybody has to do business. Everyone seems to be a spy and collaborator. There is no trust. A tailor is selling military uniforms to militants. Only a fake dream of independence is sold to the innocent Kashmiris. There is diplomatic immunity. Terrorists want that the whole of India should burn like Kashmir and they plot to bomb Jammu. It is difficult to capture and understand the traumatised psychosis of youth. Communalism gives birth to hatred which in turn makes the land fertile and favourable to the spurt of terrorism.

Shared features: A common element in all these movies is how training is imparted to small innocent children by hard-core militants. Childhood is an important age and also the learning age. The ways our thoughts are moulded have a lifetime validity. They are given guns instead of toys; they are bombarded with anger and hatred rather than love and brotherhood. This proves that the innocent are the biggest casualties of any war or conflict situation. Also, the castings of all the four movies have noise and sounds of gun-shots and bombs in the background. Anger is engrained and a whole generation of people have grown in Kashmir with hearts full of hatred and eyes full of tears. It is either against the military or militants, but the core issue is that no one has been civil to the civilians, i.e. the Kashmiris. Each of the films has strong female characters playing all shades – victim, terrorist, collaborator, citizen.

It can be reasoned like this, "I'd heard stories of how hundreds of young men – excited, idealistic teenagers; hurt, angry boys wronged by police or army action; vengeful brothers with raped sisters and mothers at home; firebrand youth leaders conjuring up paradisiacal visions of freedom and an independent Kashmir – have been leaving home everywhere and joining the Movement by walking the perilous walk across the border to receive arms and training and return as militants, as freedom fighters".[10]

Conclusion

The important question here is to achieve a full awareness concerning the Kashmir issue or the movies related to it, as both are intertwined and inseparable in the present context of this chapter. A better way to look at it is to highlight those areas which so far have been beyond the scope of Bollywood. Below the shadow of the scenic beauty of the valley, bodies of civilians remain unidentified. Mass graveyards remain unearthed and so the stories of people buried in them. Militancy was in its peak in 1990's and people were killed and many disappeared in mysterious circumstances. Civilians were abducted by either militants or the army on mere suspicion. Their families are still waiting, "half-widows" (they could not be accorded the status of widows because their husbands have been missing for years and one is not sure if the person is dead or alive) deserve answers. Anger, outrage and uncertainty have become part and parcel of people's lives. Uncertainty is the worst kind of unkindness. This part needs to be captured with much more sensitivity, research and responsibility. Past efforts have been good but there is always scope of future possibilities – both for the Kashmir issue and its portrayal in Bollywood.

---

[10] Waheed, Mirza. *The Collaborator*. New Delhi: Penguin Books India, 2011, p. 24.

The Multicultural Maze of Indian Cinema.

Shweta

A walk through the streets in any part of India, be it a village, a town or a metropolitan city, makes one confront people and localities laden with a variety of cultural traits. Visit the Chandni Chowk in Delhi, Chowpatti in Mumbai, or Vishwanath *gulli* [lane] in Varanasi, you will find glimpses of a composite culture. In India, people from a myriad of cultural backgrounds live and contribute to the larger social canvas. Men wearing a skull cap or a turban or sporting a *tilak* (a coloured mark on the forehead of men); women wearing a *saree* (the traditional Indian attire), a *burqa* (veil); some with *kumkum* (a coloured mark on the forehead of women); some people in traditional Indian attire while some in contemporary wear.

As you start noticing the cultural dimensions of the people around you, you may come across a devout Hindu vegetable seller and a Muslim tailor in the same locality. As you expand your horizon of looking and evaluate the cultural canvas of the Indian society you may notice individuals from different religions, ethnicity, class, caste, sexual orientation, and age, which are the determinants of cultural orientation of an individual, living in proximity. Each one of these individuals belongs to a larger socio-cultural space but has one's own distinct identity intact. When you look at the overall picture it becomes evident that Indian society is largely multicultural. In India Muslims, Christians, Hindus, Sikhs and persons from different races and sects live side by side in varying degrees of conflict and cooperation. The consequences of cultural proximity are complex. Multicultural settings create multiple identities and so challenge the totems of existing cultures as well as the interests of some of those within them.

Multiculturalism in its broader sense implies a phenomenon in which multiple cultures exist together. The term is used for a range of meanings, ranging from the advocacy of equal respect to the various cultures in a society. Multiculturalism is often defined as a "cultural mosaic" or a "melting pot". In contemporary society, different understandings of multiculturalism have been shaped up. One of them focuses on the interaction and communication between different cultures. Interactions of cultures or individuals create a platform in which multiculturalism is created. Multiculturalism can also be defined in terms of reaching out to both the native-born and newcomers, in developing lasting relationships among ethnic and religious communities. It encourages these communities to participate fully in society by enhancing their level of economic, social, and cultural integration into the host culture(s).[1]

Cinematic language is one of representation and reflection concerning a myriad of ideas. Film makers in any part of the world have always shown fascination towards depicting the multifaceted aspect of culture. The kaleidoscopic representation of Indian culture involves the practice of seeing through the cultural maze of Indian society and requires the identification of cultural totems and some generalisation about them: the images, meanings, norms, values, stories, and practices that seem significant in determining how political or social life look like. Cultures as depicted in films are constructed on a number of levels: in villages or cities, or across family clan, ethnic, national, religious and other networks. Hence, the identity of individuals (characters) in such films is defined by the culture which is made up of customs, norms, and genres that inform social life. There are numerous films which create, represent, discuss, magnify, and identify the cultural dynamics of human beings. The concept of multiculturalism has been dealt beautifully in a number of Indian films.

Along with multiculturalism comes the idea of representation. The notion of representation in films or any art form originates from the fact that culture forms the basic component of any individual personality. An individual from one cultural background is different from another. This difference according to Stuart Hall is essential to create meaning. Hall also says, "representation is a complex business and especially

---

[1] Murden, Simon. "Culture in World Affairs.", in Baylis John, Smith Steve and Patricia Owens. *The Globalization of World Politics*. Oxford: Oxford University Press, 2005, p. 420.

when dealing with difference it engages feelings and attitudes and emotions".[2]

What is common among some characters from three different movies? Jay and Veeru from *Sholay* (*Embers*, 1975), DJ from the movie *Rang De Basanti* (*Colour of Sacrifice*, 2006) and Mahadev from *Welcome to Sajjanpur* (2008). They are the characters of movies in which Indian society has been shown as multicultural. These are the films in which multiculturalism is written right on the face. The diversity in these films is not restricted to just nationality or ethnicity, in fact it goes even beyond the disparities of language, sexual orientation and religious customs, into regions of personal likes and dislikes. These films reach to the point in which the term diversity loses meaning and it all boils down to individuals, who are like human islands with personalised cultural traits.

Rang De Basanti is a movie which creates clash and coordination among its characters owing to their individual and cultural differences at various levels. The movie is the representation of a society in which the individuals, despite being part of a distinct separate space (one which may be classified in terms of difference concerning religion, nationality, class, sex, ideologies, etc.), are continuously involved in a dialogic process when clubbed together from a larger social space. Dialogue among the representatives of different cultural spaces is necessary for the creation of meaning. It is an important element while describing the difference between these individuals as separate entities. The Russian linguist and critic Mikhail Bakhtin argued that "meaning" is established through dialogue – it is fundamentally dialogic. Everything we say and mean is modified by the interaction and interplay with another person. Meaning arises through the "difference" between the participants in any dialogue.[3]

The movie starts with the first person narrative of a British officer in pre-independent India who is witnessing the trial of three revolutionaries. It soon turns out that the story of the film is based in post independent India and revolves around young people. Struggling

---

[2] Hall, Stuart. "Work of Representation.", in Stuart Hall (Ed.), *Representation: Cultural Representations and Signifying Practices*. New Delhi: Sage and the Open University, 1997, p. 22.
[3] Hall, Stuart. "The Spectacle of the 'Other'", in *Representation, op.cit.*, p. 235.

British filmmaker Sue McKinley comes across the diary of her grandfather, Mr. McKinley, who served as a police officer during the Indian independence movement. Through the diary, she learns about the story of five freedom fighters who were active in the movement: Chandrasekhar Azad, Bhagat Singh, Shivaram Rajguru, Ashfaqulla Khan, and Ram Prasad Bismil. McKinley, states in his diary that he had previously met two types of people in his life, the first one, who died without uttering a sound and the second kind, who died in extreme anguish, crying over their deaths. Then she reads that he finally met with the third kind who cherished his death and romanticised the idea of dying for one's own nation.

Sue lands in India and with the help of her Indian friend Sonia conducts a few unsuccessful auditions. Incidentally, she finds out that Sonia along with her friends can be the best possible cast for her documentary. Once the characters are introduced, the film goes beyond time and space, sometimes depicting the pre-independent era in the form of a docu-drama. As the movie progresses, Sue time and time again acquires the role of narrator. The film keeps pacing to and fro representing the reel life and real life of the central characters: Sonia, Aslam, DJ, Sukhi, Karan and Lakshman Pandey. The film takes a different turn when the problems of twenty-first century India are shown and how youth protest and take stand. Sonia's fiancée Ajay is killed in a fighter aircraft crash and government corruption appears to be the root cause of the incident. This event radicalises this bunch of youth from being carefree to passion-driven individuals who are determined to avenge his death.

The film represents the society and human behavior through a number of techniques. The director while making this film has used many signs and stereotyped images in order to make the inherent messages comprehensive. While depicting the multicultural set-up in *Rang De Basanti*, the projection of characters has been done in such a way that their individuality and distinctiveness does not escape the notice of the audience. The characters in the film are representative of various cultural spaces. Sue is a foreigner. She is most of the time intrigued by the manner in which Indians work and behave. The important thing in her representation is the breaking of the cultural and geopolitical boundary as she is comfortable in speaking Hindi. Karan is another character who is representative of the higher class. He comes from the affluent society. His father is a businessman having connections in political circles. Aslam is a moderate Muslim boy and comes from an orthodox Muslim family. As far as Aslam is concerned he has a different approach towards life, which is not governed by religious sentiments but by rationale.

A contrast has been drawn between Aslam and his family. Aslam's house is located in a Muslim-populated area. His brother wears a skull cap. Both his father and his brother have grudges against Indian society and the government. They both hold this view that Muslims being in minority have still not been given their fair share in India. They have still not been accepted by the majority, i.e., the Hindu population, which includes the major part of the political and social machinery. Aslam is slammed by his family, especially his father and brother, for having friendship with non-Muslims. The women in his household are subservient to the male. The depiction of his household is in accordance with the long-held belief about Muslim colonies [homogeneous areas of residence] and families. The representation of Aslam's family can best be explained in terms of difference and the dialogue with the "Other". In the words of Hall, "The argument here is that we need difference because we can only construct meaning through a dialogue with the 'Other'".[4]

Another character is DJ (Daljeet) from a Sikh family. DJ's mother runs a food joint. She is a tall, fair and healthy woman with long hair and speaks fluent Punjabi (the language spoken by Sikhs). Her portrayal is of a conventional Sikh woman. DJ's grandfather is an old man with a beard who wears a turban. He has been portrayed as a religious man who rises early in the morning to perform his prayers. The representation is of a typical Sikh man and woman, which can be explained in terms of the general characteristic of stereotyping. In the words of Hall, "We understand the world by referring individual objects, people or events in our heads to general classificatory schemes into which - according to our culture - they fit".[5] Lakshman Pandey is another character who is a party activist in a Hindu political organisation. Lakshman Pandey and company are shown as anti-western workers who protest against anything which "supposedly" is a

[4] Hall, Stuart. "The Spectacle of the 'Other'.", in *Representation, op.cit.*, p. 235.
[5] *Ibid.*, p. 257.

threat to Indian culture. Lakshman Pandey keeps a saffron stole around his neck and puts a *tilak* on his forehead. Both the *tilak* and the saffron stole symbolise a right wing political orientation. Hall says, "the underlying argument behind the semiotic approach is that, since all cultural objects convey meaning, they must make use of signs".[6]

Initially, due to his anti-Muslim beliefs and contempt for Aslam, he is unpopular in the group but later on, when he joins the cast of the documentary he finds a place among them. The film also represents the ever changing trajectory of the relationship between Aslam and Lakshman Pandey, one which is at first tangibly grounded on hostility but later the equations change and owing to dialogue the differences evaporate. The other characters Sukhi, Ajay and Sonia have been sketched rather than fully portrayed. All the characters, how different they may be, at one point form a single social unit. At one point the line differentiating them starts dissolving and they become part of a larger social structure with their individualities still intact. Sometimes in the form of a melting pot, as in the case of all the friends, and sometimes to represent a cultural mosaic as in the case of their families, the social set-up in this film has been portrayed as multicultural.

In the movie *Welcome to Sajjanpur*, Mahadev Kushwaha is an unemployed graduate who lives in a village named Sajjanpur and earns his living by writing letters for others. He wants to become a novel writer. His mother is a vegetable seller. Their household is a perfect rural Hindu household. Among Mahadev's customers are: Mahadev's childhood love Kamla, who is desperate because she has no news from her husband Bansi Ram. Kamla is a simple village girl, who lives with her mother-in-law. She is a *kumharin* (potter). Her husband Bansi Ram works as a labourer at a dockyard in Mumbai. In the letters to her husband, a jealous Mahadev writes the opposite of the loving messages Kamla wants to convey.

Another of his customers is a village middle-aged woman, who wants to get her *manglik* (having ominous horoscope) daughter, Vindhya, married. A landlord, whose wife is a candidate for the village *Sarpanch* [Head of village], wants to eliminate all her political rivals from the race. A eunuch, Munni, is contesting the elections for the

---

[6] Hall, Stuart. "Work of Representation.", in *Representation, op.cit.*, p. 59.

village *Sarpanch* but fears the threats from the landlord. A compounder, Ram Kumar, another customer of Mahadev, falls in love with his daughter-in-law Shobha Rani, the widow of a retired army soldier. A snake charmer who is in search of his missing father also has his letters written by Mahadev. Another customer is a superstitious man, who tells Mahadev to write a hundred letters to avoid a bad omen. The place where Mahadev sits and writes the letters is surrounded by a general store, a tailor's shop, a mechanic's shop, a tea shop. A postman is also often seen going around the area. Through his humble occupation, Mahadev has the potential to affect numerous lives. The movie is a satirical but warm-hearted portrait of life in rural India. Mahadev manages to get his friend the compounder engaged, arranges police protection for Munni who is contesting in an election against all odds, and almost wins Kamla's heart until one day he finds a shocking truth about Kamla's husband. Munni wins the local election but is later killed. As the movie approaches its end, it soon turns out that the story was a fictional novel written by the real Mahadev, mostly based on his own experiences.

The village is a set-up where a number of individuals from different backgrounds and values are living and earning their livelihood through various means. They have their own identities. Each character along with the protagonist carries a set of meanings because of his/her representation. There is a story, a problem associated with each of them. Whether it is Mahadev, Kamla, Munni, the postman, Salim Mohammad, the snake charmer, or the compounder Ram Kumar, all of them have a distinct characteristic. Their dressing sense, values, habits, orientation, ethnic or religious background vary from each other. Yet they together are part of a single society. The movie also shows clash and coordination among these individual entities. The clash for power has been shown at the village level. In the fray for the election concerning the post of village head are involved: the village landlord's wife, the eunuch Munnibai and Rehmet ul nisa, the wife of another villager, Salim Mohammad. The landlord conspires against both the rival candidates and succeeds in the dismissal of the candidature of Rehmet ul nisa on the grounds that her husband is a Pakistani agent. Munni somehow manages to save her own candidature and later wins the election. The complaint lodged by the landlord against Salim Mohammad describing him as a Pakistani agent is a satire on the face of our social and political set-up. It is ironical that in spite of having been part of Indian society for so long, Muslims are accused of being against India and many a time are penalised by the police and the administration. The character of Munni is also significant as it reflects the gross inequalities prevalent in Indian society. Even as Indian constitution prohibits discrimination on the basis of caste, creed, religion and sex and has given equal rights to all its citizens, eunuchs in India are still devoid of their rights. This is largely due to the anomalies in both social and political machinery. Our society has still not given acceptance to them and the administration is blindfolded towards their needs. The film also depicts the element of superstition magnificently, be it Vindhya's mother or the man who comes to get a hundred letters written in order to avoid the bad omen.

A clash of beliefs has been shown between Vindhya and her mother. Vindhya is an educated girl who believes in spending her life in her own way, while her mother is a finicky woman who is still stuck to superstitious beliefs. Vindhya and her mother are part of a society in which younger generations live with the older ones in spite of individual and philosophical differences. Other women characters in the movie display varied degrees of the cultural disparities which exist in society. Shobha Rani, a widow, falls in love with the village compounder Ram Kumar. This love affair raises the issue of widow remarriage, one which is still unacceptable in many parts of the country. Young Kamla has been waiting for her husband for four years and is not sure when she will be able to meet him. Her solitude is broken when she comes across her childhood friend Mahadev, but before she can break her virtuous barrier the film takes a different turn. Kamla's story shows the plight of women in India, who even when abandoned by their husbands are tied with their marital status. The movie ardently deals with a variety of women characters and shows how as individuals they contribute to the larger cultural platter.

The film shows a composite framework in which each individual is a cultural unit in itself, one defined by totems, boundaries and religious affiliations. It depicts multiculturalism as both descriptive and normative. Descriptive refers to cultural diversity, while normative implies a positive endorsement, even the celebration, of communal diversity, typically based on either the right of different groups to respect and recognition or on the alleged benefits to the larger society depending on moral and cultural diversity.[7] The movie depicts the society as a cultural mosaic, in which, people from different cultural backgrounds exist together in a social set-up. Each individual has its own identity, its own lifestyle, its own totems and influences on the basis of which his/her life is governed. The defining features of the individuals who are parts of a cultural mosaic are their distinct identities.

In *Sholay*, the element of multiculturalism has been depicted beautifully and subtly. The movie is exciting, fascinating and revolutionised in its own way the conventions of the "commercial" Hindi film; it oscillates with regularity between moments of extreme tension and instants of tenderness. The film includes scenes of fights between opposite groups as well as of one-to-one combat, sadistic bandits supposedly meting out justice in their own way, the heroes are petty criminals just out of prison, but finally turn out to be full of noble sentiments. These two, Veeru and Jaidev, have been recruited as mercenaries by an ex-police officer (Thakur) who had seen them defend their train from attacking bandits when he was taking them to prison. This ex-policeman (Thakur) is a landowner in an isolated village, whose entire family has been murdered by the bandit Gabbar Singh.

In another grisly incident Thakur's two arms are cut off by Gabbar Singh. It is revenge and not the forces of law and order which motivate Thakur to hire these two men to get rid of the bandit. The film also has two love stories: one, in a light and sardonic tone, between Veeru and the village girl Basanti and the other, a tragic one of the second hero, Jai, with the widowed daughter-in-law of the Thakur. In its course, the film also sticks to the proverbial picture of communal harmony by showing the wonderful relations between the villagers and the old blind Muslim priest (Imam) of the little village mosque. While fighting Gabbar Singh, Jai is killed. Finally Gabbar Singh is captured and his gang either killed or captured.[8] Concerning the death of Jai, Yves Thoraval says, "Jai's death, not a common occurrence for a 'positive' hero, seems to be the solution to a thorny moral problem – widow

---

[7] [http://en.wikipedia.org/wiki/Multiculturalism, accessed 5 October 2011].
[8] Thoraval, Yves. "1960-1990: Escapism Formulas and the Star System.", in Yves Thoraval, *The Cinemas of India*. Delhi: Macmillan India, 2000, pp. 123-124.

remarriage not being an acceptable practice for orthodox Hindus and something the public might not have been happy with".[9]

The village, Ramgarh, where the entire action takes place is located in the midst of rocky mountains. The village community consists of a number of individuals from different cultures, religions, sexes, classes and occupations. Each one of them has a defined pattern of life. The village has a mosque and a temple. The Hindus in the village share a unique relationship with the Muslim priest (Imam). This cooperation is shown often by Basanti meeting the Imam now and then. Sometimes helping him and sometimes convincing his son about various issues which the Imam could not impress upon him. The portrayal of the Imam who wears a skull cap and keeps a beard is a perfect example of stereotyping. Though no conflict has been shown between the villagers, who are mostly Hindus, and the Imam, his portrayal certainly delivers the inherent attitude of stereotyping the "Other". Hence it imprints symbolically fixed boundaries, i.e., a Muslim will always be shown wearing a skull cap, and excluding everything which does not belong to this fraternity.

Ramgarh cannot be termed a classless village. Although there is harmony among the villagers, the village has a well-defined class structure. The ex-policeman Thakur belongs to the land-owning class. He lives in a *haveli* [mansion] and has more than sufficient money. Drawing a contrast to the position held by Thakur there are the villagers who are either small land-owning farmers, shopkeepers or engaged in some occupation (blacksmith, potter, washerman, etc.). But what is significant here is the fact that all the villagers together as a social unit are against the bandits. The multicultural portrayal of the village community is incomplete without the two main women characters Basanti and Radha. Basanti is a *tangewali* (horse cart rider), who earns her living by transporting villagers from one place to another. The work she is engaged in is not a conventional one for women. The film through the portrayal of Basanti breaks the normative standards of depicting a woman in a rural set-up. Another woman character is Radha who is a widow. Radha wears a white saree and is silent in the entire movie. Although Radha falls in love with Jai, throughout the movie she has been cordoned off by an invisible line. Thakur agrees to her

---

[9] *Ibid.*, p. 124.

remarriage but she is left alone as Jai dies in the fight with Gabbar Singh. Radha in the end remains in her white saree which has become synonymous to and symbolizes the status of a widow in Indian society.

Hall says, "Stereotyping deploys a strategy of 'spilling'. It divides the normal and the acceptable from the abnormal and the unacceptable. It then excludes or expels everything which does not fit; which is different".[10] Largely the movie depicts the multicultural backgrounds in which a number of individuals with varying degrees of cultural, occupational and other orientation are living together. All the three movies are based in different locations and have different issues under consideration. The characters in these movies are quite different but at one level some common elements may be found in their representation. Stereotyping is also evident in all the three films. The portrayal of Muslims can clearly be classified as stereotyping. In all these movies, Muslims are shown wearing a skull cap and having a beard. In *Rang De Basanti* and *Welcome to Sajjanpur* elements of both clash and coordination are shown in the interaction between Muslims, (in minority and subordinate in terms of power) with Hindus, the majority. Hall links such portrayal to power equations and says, "stereotyping tends to occur where there are gross inequalities of power. Power is usually directed against the subordinate or excluded group".[11]

As far as the depiction of a woman is considered, the three movies have diversified approaches. But what is common in all these movies is that even as their shades of character are different they are part of a larger canvas; each of them has a different colour but together they form a picture, in which each colour is important. Multiculturalism is engrained in each of these three movies. The society has been depicted as a larger social unit in which individuals from a myriad of cultural spaces interact among one another; their differences shown in terms of conflict and coordination, when clubbed together represent a multicultural society.

---

[10] Hall, Stuart. "The Spectacle of the 'Other'.", in *Representation, op.cit.*, p. 258.
[11] *Ibid.*

Sexuality Minorities in Indian Society and their Portrayal in Bollywood Cinema.

Sudarshan Yadav

In the initial years of cinema female characters were played by male actors. It thereby gave a manly touch to feminine characters, though the main reason was because at that time women were reluctant to act in films. This peculiar feature does not strictly concern sexuality minorities; however, it is worth observing how at the time audiences watched feminine characters with manly features. So, this article looks into the issue concerning the representation of "sexuality minorities" in Bollywood films. Here the term "sexuality minorities" has been used to cater to the broader area of sexuality in which people are discriminated against, owing to their sexual identity/orientation or gender identity. This includes gays, lesbians, bisexuals, *hijras* [eunuchs, from an Arabic/Urdu word meaning separation], *kothis* [people regarded as feminine men, not living however in communities], transgenders, etc.[1] While discussing the different reasons responsible for the plight of eunuchs, transgenders or homosexuals in society, it further considers the portrayal of eunuchs with reference to three Bollywood films. These films are *Darmiyaan* (*In-Between*, 1997), *Tamanna* (*Wish*, 1997) and *Shabnam Mausi* (*Aunt Shabnam*, 2005). All these films present different issues related to the condition of eunuchs in society, along with strong comments on why and what "they" have to suffer in society. These films try to break the image of eunuchs as stored in the minds of people, by laying emphasis on the fact that even eunuchs are humans.

The prominent presentation of eunuchs in Bollywood cinema came with eunuchs singing a "*badhai*" (congratulating) song to Mahmood for

---

[1] PUCL-K Report. "Human Rights Violation against Sexuality Minorities in India.", in *PUCL-K 2001*. Web 6 February 2001 [http://www.sangama.org/files/sexual-minorities.pdf, accessed 10 August 2011].

getting a son in *Kunwara Baap* (*Unmarried Father*, 1974). Also, *Mughal-e-Azam* (*Mughal King*, 1960) had a eunuch in the harem of the king. Since it was a historical film, the presence of a eunuch was but natural. Later on, there were no real portrayals of eunuchs in particular or sexual minorities broadly, excepting stereotyped roles of dancers or singers, as in the film *Amar Akbar Anthony* (1977). The very popular song *Mere Angne Me Tumhara Kya Kaam Hai* (*In my house what purpose do you serve*) in the film *Lawaris* (*Bastard*, 1981) presents Amitabh Bachchan cross-dressing as a eunuch and making fun about husband-wife relationship. But, the very first presentation of eunuchs in actual filmic roles occurred in *Sadak* (*Road*, 1991). Since then many films presenting sexuality minorities got released in mainstream Bollywood cinema and other regional cinemas too. Some of the prominent films are *Daayra* (*The Square Circle*, 1996), *Fire* (1996), *Darmiyaan* (1997), *Tamanna* (1997), *Nayak: The Real Hero* (2001), *Kal Ho Naa Ho* (*Whether Tomorrow Comes or Not*, 2003), *Girlfriend* (2004), *Masti* (*Mischief: Oath on Beloved*, 2004), *Kyaa Kool Hain Hum* (*How Cool We Are*, 2005), *Maine Pyaar Kyun Kiya* (*Why I Have Fallen in Love*, 2005), *My Brother...Nikhil* (2005), *Shabnam Mausi* (2005), *Water* (2005), *Honeymoon Travels Private Ltd.* (2007), *Dostana* (*Friendship*, 2008), *Welcome to Sajjanpur* (2008), *Dunno Y Na Jaane Kyun* (*Don't Know Why*, 2010), *Housefull* (2010), etc. This way, the society got an access to the world which is "Other" and also considered taboo, so as to promote a change in the usual perspective.

Presentation of the Sexuality Minorities in Bollywood Cinema

The films mentioned earlier can be put into four different categories in terms of the presentation of the characters. This presentation is based on their filmic structure. Those are:

As Cameo/Character Role

The term cameo is used for a well-known artist who appears in a film for a very short role. The sole purpose of this presence is to help the protagonist achieve his/her goal. In some films this role is played by the eunuchs/transgenders, although the actors playing them may not be well known, they certainly help the protagonist. Nowadays eunuchs constitute a more integral part of the plot. The films with this kind of presentation are: *Mughal-e-Azam* (1960), *Amar Akbar Anthony* (1977),

Bombay (1995), *Maine Dil Tujhko Diya* (*I Have Given My Heart To You*, 2002), *Page* 3 (2005), *Honeymoon Travels Private Ltd.* (2007), *Fashion* (2008), *Jodhaa Akbar* (2008), *Welcome to Sajjanpur* (2008), etc. In the film *Amar Akbar Anthony* there is a song sequence *Taiyaab Ali Pyaar ka Dushman, Haay Haay* (*Taiyaab Ali, The Enemy of Love, Disgrace to you*); in this song a group of eunuchs helps Akbar (Rishi Kapoor) to tackle and bring disgrace publicly to Taiyyab Ali, the father of the girl whom Akbar loves. The film *Bombay* (1995) directed by Mani Ratnam shows a eunuch taking out of danger in a riot the son of the protagonist. While the other people are concerned with religious communalism, the eunuch saves the child irrespective of the religion. In the case of *Mughal-e-Azam* and *Jodhaa Akbar*, which are historical films dealing with the Mughals period, eunuchs appear in the harems of the king.

In terms of character role, *Maine Dil Tujhko Diya* has a character named Bobby Darling. He is a student in the same college where the protagonist studies. He is ridiculed and mocked in the film for his sexuality, yet he helps the protagonist to earn money in his need. He gives a *mangalsutra* (the sacred thread that a married woman wears in Hindu culture) to the protagonist, so that he can marry the girl he loves. *Welcome to Sajjanpur* has a eunuch character named *Munnibai Mukhanni*. This eunuch is contesting elections for the village *Sarpanch* (Head). The local landlord threatens and tells the eunuch not to contest the elections. She refuses and is murdered. *Fashion* and *Page 3* have been directed by Madhur Bhandarkar. In *Fashion* there are two fashion designers, one is gay and the other one is bisexual. They help the protagonist, Priyanka Chopra, to regain her stature of super model in the fashion industry. In *Page 3* there is an upcoming actor who is the boyfriend of the protagonist, Konkana Sen. He indulges in a relationship with one of the friends of Konkana who is gay.

As Entertainment Filler

Here the purpose of including sexuality minorities in the script is to inject some entertainment elements so that the story won't become heavy. This way of presenting sexuality minorities in films is in vogue. Mostly in such case, the characters are portrayed in a ridiculing manner and mocked all through the film. The films of this category are: *Maine*

Pyar Kiya (*My Love Kiya*, 1989), *Chamatkar* (*Miracle*, 1992), *Pyaar Kiya To Darna Kya* (*When in Love, No Need to Worry*, 1998), *Ghulam* (*Slave*, 1998), *Ab Tak Chhappan* (*Till Now Fifty-six*, 2004), *Masti* (*Mischief: Oath on Beloved*, 2004), *Kyaa Kool Hain Hum* (*How Cool We Are*, 2005), etc.

As Protagonist

As far as eunuchs are concerned in mainstream Bollywood cinema there are very few films portraying them as protagonists. Some of these films are *Darmiyaan, Tamanna* and *Shabnam Mausi*. Nowadays films portraying homosexual relationships and characters are also being produced by Bollywood. The film *Fire* features the relationship (lesbian) of two sisters-in-law and the circumstances under which that relationship happened. *My Brother Nikhil* is another film presenting the issue of HIV-AIDS in which the protagonist (a budding sportsperson) gets this disease through a homosexual relation. This film subtly presents the issue of homosexual identity with focus on the suffering of an AIDS victim. Recently a film *Dunno Y Na Jaane Kyun* on a gay relationship has been released in India. This is the first film in the history of Indian cinema portraying a gay relationship openly with a man to man smooch. Earlier a film, *Girlfriend* was released starring Isha Koppikar and Amrita Arora presenting the issue of a lesbian relationship. This film attributed the reason for getting into lesbian relationships to mental and psychological disorders.

As Antagonist

There are films in which sexual minorities are presented directly or indirectly as antagonists. The film *Sadak* by Mahesh Bhatt started this trend. In *Sadak*, Sadashiva Amrapurkar appeared as Maharani. Later on, a few other films like *Karam* (*Deeds*, 2005), *Ek Chalis Ki Last Local* (*The Last Local of One Forty*, 2007) have characters with a negative role. *Karam* features a eunuch underworld don. In the film *Ek Chalis Ki Last Local* there are two characters, a gay underworld don and a eunuch who is a mistress of prostitutes. But in this case the mistress helps the protagonist by lending him money on the request of the prostitute (Neha Dhupia) who works under the mistress. There are no sexual minorities as characters in the film, *Sangharsh* (*Struggle*, 1999) directed by Tanuja Chandra. In one of the scenes, the antagonist, Ashutosh Rana (a psychic), abducts a kid and in order to keep his identity from getting

revealed dresses him as a woman. However, he is generally presented in
the film as if he were a eunuch.

Three Films, One Issue

The three films to be discussed in this article are *Tamanna,
Darmiyaan* and *Shabnam Mausi*. The first two films are fictional stories
based on true incidents, while *Shabnam Mausi* is more of a biographical
account with elements of fiction about the first eunuch to be elected as
Member of Legislature in India, Shabnam Bano.

In the film *Tamanna* directed by Mahesh Bhatt, an extradiegetic
(omniscient narrator, external to the story) introduces the film and takes
the audience to the past in the year 1975. Here, the analepsis (going
back in time) occurs with the prolepsis (contrary of analepsis, future in
time) as the story moves on in the future, the time when this film was
released, i.e., in the year 1997. This film deals with the story of a
eunuch (Tikku) son of a great actress of the past. He finds a newly-born
girl child in the garbage and adopts her as his own daughter. As time
passes the girl grows old, and comes to know that this person whom she
calls Abbu (Father) is a eunuch but not his real father. So she searches
for her real parents and finds that her real father (Thakur Ranvir
Chopra) dislikes girl children. This hatred resulted in the killing of two
other girls at their births. Later on in the film, Tamanna gives a DNA
report to her real father that proves his paternity. This results in an
attempt by her real father to kill Tamanna, but she is rescued by her
Abbu (Tikku) and the eunuch clan.

In this film, the plight of eunuchs is shown, i.e., what they have to
suffer in their day to day struggle for existence. At the same time it
portrays the other side of the eunuchs longing to have love and to be
loved. This other side actually keeps care of the girl child (Tamanna)
that our patriarchal society does not accept. The notion that eunuchs are
impure and should be excluded from society and human sympathy has
been beautifully portrayed in the film, when Tamanna finds that Tikku
is a eunuch. In this scene, Tamanna says, "Who is this man? I don't
know him? He is a eunuch. I feel like vomiting when I think that once
he has touched me, once he has fed me". This scene indicates how the
prejudice nurtured by society outshines the good deeds of the eunuch

(Tikku), who has striven hard to protect Tamanna and has given her good education and life. This cultural imprint presents 'them' as taboo and impure. In another scene when Tikku asks his step brother for money, the latter addresses him as eunuch (*Naznin ka hijda*) and does not give him a penny. This forces Tikku to join the eunuch clan, where he has to sing and dance for his earning. There is a scene in which Tikku laments over not knowing English as it has resulted in losing his job. This introduces the issue of the non-education of eunuchs in our society.

On the other hand, one can say that the film *Darmiyaan* directed by Kalpana Lajmi is the extension in the past of the story of *Tamanna*. *Tamanna* starts with the eunuch finding a child while *Darmiyaan* ends with the eunuch finding a child and committing suicide along with his mother. *Darmiyaan* also deals with the story of a *hijra* (Immi, played by Arif Zakaria) who is the son of a great actress from the past. This film tells the story of the eunuch, Immi, who sees the downfall of his mother from a superstar actress to a bankrupt woman. The actress loses her mind and the responsibility of taking care falls on Immi. Since society and even his own father are not able to help him, Immi is forced to join the eunuch clan, where he earns money by singing and dancing. One day Immi is gang raped and life has no meaning for him; however, he finds in a child a ray of hope. But the head of the eunuch clan (Champa) is about to castrate that child, who is rescued by Immi. He finally gives the child to the leading actress of that time Chitra (Tabu). This film is an extradiegetic narration that starts in the year 1946 (analepsis) covering the life of Immi till the 1960s. A prolepsis occurs from 1946 to 1960s, but the film got released in 1997. So the story is from the past itself. In between an ellipsis (to skip some time) of 12 years occurs, when the story shifts from the childhood of Immi (1946) to his adulthood (1958). This is covered in just a few minutes.

In this film there is a song, *Apne Desh Me Hum Hain Pardeshi* (In my own land, I'm an outsider). This song portrays the pain and agony of the eunuchs. It starts with the lyrics *Kaisa Gham Hai Kya Majboori Hai, Paas Hain Jo Unse Bhi Doori Hai, Dil Yun Tadpe Jaise Koi Gunga Bolna Chahe, Lekin Sab Hain Anjane.* (What kind of sorrow is this, what is the reason for this helplessness; even those who are close to us are far away from us, the heart suffers as if someone who is dumb would speak, but everyone does not know this). While these lines are sung in the film, the scene of the mother and the son is shown. In this scene, the son (Immi about 10 years old) is lying on the lap of his mother (Kirron Kher) when he comes to know that she is her mother, rather than *Aapa* (sister). When Immi calls her *Ammi* (mother), she insists that he should call her *Aapa* only. So the pain of Immi (a eunuch) is brilliantly portrayed through these lines in the song where his identity is not even totally accepted by his family group including the mother. This non-acceptance is also portrayed in another scene, one in which Immi's father (Javed Bhai, a film studio owner) rescues Immi from the people who are beating and ridiculing him. In this scene, Javed Bhai in a slip of tongue is about to tell that Immi is his son, but restrains himself from uttering that word and says Immi is my brother-in-law. Further on, when Javed Bhai introduces Immi to his son, he says, *Immi, inse milo ye hain Salim, mere iklaute bete* (Immi meet Salim, my only son). This scene clearly presents the reluctance of the father to accept that he is a father of a eunuch (or in common terms one can say father of a "*Chakka*", i.e., an impotent one).

Shabnam Mausi, directed by Yogesh Bharadwaj, features an extradiegetic narration that starts with frames of eunuch life (real footages from Mumbai). It also moves back in time (analepsis), followed by a prolepsis reaching the year 2002. An ellipsis takes place when Shabnam is about 5 years old and in the next scene she is shown as a fully grown adult (almost an ellipsis of 20 years). Later in the film an ellipsis occurs again in the change of the make-up of the character Shabnam (mature look). The extradiegetic narration becomes clear when the narrator links diegetically the running away of Shabnam from the police in order to reach Anooppur in Madhya Pradesh. This film presents the sufferings and pain of eunuchs through the eyes of a eunuch herself who will become the first Member of Legislature in the history of India. It is a fiction film based on the biographical details of Shabnam Bano. There is a short story of Lolo (friend of Shabnam) who was married to a king to safeguard his harem. There is an argument by Shabnam that eunuchs left the society to become saints, sufis and fakirs. But the involvement of some of the eunuchs in sex work has brought a bad name to the community, a feeling which has culminated in the outcasting of the eunuchs from society. The problem of education and jobs has also been presented in the film. Here the government official says *agde ko do, picchde ko do, ab hijde ko bhi do*, meaning till now we were giving jobs to upper class, even to lower class but now we have to give jobs to eunuchs also? Uttering these words he throws Shabnam out of his office. This reflects the mindset of the larger section of society.

The self-pity and pain among eunuchs is also reflected in these three films. In *Tamanna*, Tikku asks his daughter what is my fault in being a *hijda*, my existence is because of God's will. When Tikku's step brother ill-treats him, Salim Bhai (Manoj Bajpai) cries. Reacting to this Tikku says it is really nice to see that someone in this world is crying for me. In *Shabnam Mausi*, Shabnam talks to her mother (Halima) and asks why we are outcasts, when society does not outcast the childless mothers and impotent males. In the case of *Darmiyaan* too, the self-pity of the character is featured in by this song, *Koi bata de hum kyun zinda hain, hum yun khud se bhi sharminda hain, apni hi aankhoin se gire hain banke hum ek aansu, mane koi ya nahi mane*, (Someone would tell me why am I alive, I am so ashamed of myself, I have fallen in my eyes, which is visible in the form of tears, whether someone believes or not). In this scene, a prostitute humiliates Immi when she finds out in bed that he is a eunuch.

The humiliations and the sufferings lead eunuchs to lose hope for their lives. To establish their existence they desperately need a reason to live and survive. This is presented again in the mentioned song of *Darmiyaan*. It says, *Koi to jeene ka bahana ho* (there should be any reason to live), *koi wada ho jo nibhana ho* (there should be any promise to keep), *koi safar* (any journey) *koi to rasta* (any path) *koi to manzil ho* (any destination to reach). When these lines are sung in the film Immi finds a child in the garbage after he has been gang raped. The same desperation appears in the film, *Shabnam Mausi*, through a song, *Aa ja re Nindiyaa* meaning *Come O' Sleep*. In the case of the film *Tamanna* Tikku finds the girl child and says to Salim Bhai, this girl is my reason to live, a Tamanna (wish) of my life. All these three films, while dealing with the different issues and problems eunuchs have to suffer, try to show the human aspect of eunuchs; their aspirations, dreams, desire to be loved and to love, and most importantly not to be ridiculed by society because of their sexual identity.

Representation and Stereotyping

"Representation connects meaning and language to culture".[2] Language or signs are coded by different cultural societies differently. It is society which decides or fixes the code in a language. So, "representation is the production of the meaning of the concepts in our minds through language".[3] It can be further stated that "it is the link between concepts and language which enables us to refer to either the 'real' world of objects, people or events, or indeed to imaginary worlds".[4] The representation of sexuality minorities in Bollywood cinema is being discussed here; i.e., actually how they are presented in films. Cinema is a medium through which the language of sound, words and images is created. Representation of eunuchs or homosexuals in films is largely reflective of the way they are seen in society; mostly as a laughing stock, with a hoarse voice, an ugly appearance, a very cheap and bright make-up, with feminine modes of expression and hand clapping. These are the clichés in which the sexuality minorities are presented in media. This cliché is fixed by the "phenomenon of naturalization, where the difference is fixed and secured forever".[5] The clichés in the field of cultural studies are known as stereotypes and stereotyping. "Stereotyping reduces people to a few simple, essential characteristics which are represented as fixed by Nature".[6] Thus, the stereotyping of sexuality minorities in the films has been put broadly into five categories. The categories are:

1. *Appearance*: Eunuchs are shown to wear bright coloured clothes with cheap make-up; the obsession of jewellery along with manly body features; and having a peculiar hoarse voice. Gay men are shown to wear female clothes with feminity in their appearance.

---

[2] Hall, Stuart. "Work of Representation.", in Stuart Hall (Ed.), *Representation: Cultural Representations and Signifying Practices*. New Delhi: Sage and the Open University, 1997, p. 15.

[3] *Ibid*, p. 17.

[4] *Ibid*.

[5] Hall, Stuart. "The Spectacle of the 'Other'.", in *Representation, op.cit.*, p. 245.

[6] *Ibid.*, p. 257.

2. *Behaviour*: Hand clapping, teasing others, very blunt in their comments, cursing others when ill-treated, forcefully asking for money; these are some of the stereotypes in which eunuchs are presented in films. All the films discussed earlier have these elements. Homosexuals are portrayed as people who tease other men when they find them sexy, chew their lips as a sign of desire for other men, also flaunt feminity in their gestures and their way of talking. Lesbians are very sparingly shown in Hindi films. Still, they are mostly represented as obsessed with other women. Ex: *Girlfriend*.

3. *Being Lucky/The Blessed Ones or Their Curse Can Cause Ills*: In almost every film that has eunuch characters, it seems to be essential to show that their blessings are considered lucky by society. This is either reflected by dialogues or through symbolic codes. Some of the prominent examples are *Maine Pyar Kiya*, *Chamatkar*, *Shabnam Mausi*, *Tamanna*, etc.

Shabnam Mausi has a scene which can serve as a good example for this. In that scene Madan Pandit (a contract killer) who is about to die, stops Shabnam Mausi from blessing him for life. He says, "your blessings can save me but I want to die." In the same film Amma blesses Shabnam and says today a *hijra* is blessing a *hijra* to become the messiah for us.

The other notion that if a eunuch curses it causes ill is well portrayed in *Darmiyaan*. In one scene Champa (a eunuch) curses Immi's mother (the actress) on receiving ill-treatment from her. Ironically this notion gets established at the end of the film with the destruction of the heroine. Again in the climax of the film Immi curses Champa. He says "by the power of being a born *hijra* I curse you to be a *hijra* for your next lives too".

4. *Societal Conception*: Since sexuality minorities do not belong to the socially accepted norms of sex, therefore, they are symbolically and physically made outcasts by society. Thus, there is a veil that stops society to see "them" from another perspective. Also, due to this veil, it is quite impossible to achieve an external and unbiased awareness of the real inner life and beliefs of a eunuch. These conceptions are mostly negative.

Some of the images of eunuchs or homosexuals as conceived by society and presented in films are as follows:

- They are criminals. Ex: *Sadak, Karam*, etc.
- They abduct children and castrate them; offer children to their deities in doing rituals. Ex: *Darmiyaan, Sangharsh*.
- They are involved in sex work. Ex: *Ek Chalis Ki Last Local, Shabnam Mausi*.
- Being homosexual or bisexual is a disorder. Ex: *Kyaa Kool Hain Hum, Girlfriend*.

5. *Laughing Stock*: Lastly, eunuchs and homosexuals are always presented as a laughing stock. They act in certain stereotyped ways to invoke laughter within the film which gets transferred finally to the audience. This way of stereotyping has been used universally in all the films that have been discussed earlier in this article. There were some films in which the protagonist or some other character stops people from ridiculing them. Ex: *Maine Dil Tujhko Diya, Pyaar Kiya To Darna Kya*, etc.

Reversing Stereotypes

Apart from the above stereotyped portrayals there has also been an attempt to give new definitions to sexuality minorities. This is largely to break the existing stereotypes and reintroduce or redefine these people. In this regard it is important the portrayal of sexuality minorities as protagonists or lead characters. This perspective comes from the modernist cinema which "questions its power of the gaze, questions its power of representation (among other things reality, sexuality, ...). It questions how it represents and what it represents".[7] "Some modernist cinema, within its formal probing and experimentation, also addressed questions of subjectivity and sexuality".[8]

So, there came an attempt to add positive images to the existing stereotyped ones, such as even "they" are humans. Even the "others" have their other side, which has love and compassion for the world in spite of how the world treats "them". This new trend also minimises the

---

[7] Hayward, Susan. "Modernism.", in *Key Concepts in Cinema Studies*. London: Routledge, 2004, p. 237.
[8] *Ibid.*, p. 239.

apprehensions of society about "them". The films which fall in this category are *Darmiyaan, Tamanna, Shabnam Mausi, Daayra, My Brother...Nikhil, Honeymoon Travels Private Ltd., Fashion,* etc.

Summing Up

Summing it up, sexuality minorities started to get space in media after the '90s. Early '90s can be said as the watershed years from which sexuality minorities started to get space in media. During this time a great deal of events happened apart from the liberalisation of Indian economy and the advent of the cable TV. Among those events, the first gay magazine started in India, viz., *Bombay Dost* in June 1990.[9] In the year 1988, a major media coverage was given to the marriage of two police women Leela and Urmila.[10] "In 1991, Amnesty International for the first time came out with a policy to support the rights of people imprisoned because of their sexual orientation or because of engaging in homosexual activity in private".[11] In the mid-'90s some of the remarkable and historical changes started to happen in Tasmania, Scandinavia, and South Africa in terms of homosexual rights and prohibition of discrimination on the grounds of sexual orientation.[12]

In this regard, as Hall puts it, in the Cultural Studies, "the 'Others' who are in some way different or is out of place are considered polluted, dangerous, taboo. Negative feelings cluster around them. They must be symbolically excluded if the 'purity' of the culture is to be restored".[13] This exclusion happens in society but in the media too. "Here the practice of symbolic violence is done by the one who is in power; one who has the power to represent someone or something in a certain way".[14] This scene is largely changing with the organisations promoting the rights of the homosexuals and eunuchs, and even the inclusion of large number of sexuality minorities in different media.

---

[9] PUCL-K Report. "Human Rights Violation against Sexuality Minorities in India.", in *PUCL-K 2001*. Web 23 February 2001 [http://www.sangama.org/files/sexual-minorities.pdf, accessed 10 August 2011].

[10] *Ibid.*

[11] *Ibid.* Web 7 February 2001 [http://www.sangama.org/files/sexual-minorities.pdf, accessed 10 August 2011].

[12] *Ibid.*

[13] Hall, Stuart. "The Spectacle of the 'Other'.", in *Representation, op.cit.*, p. 258.

[14] *Ibid.*, p. 259.

In the year 1993, *Philadelphia*, a film covering the issue of gay rights got released world over. In this film, the protagonist, Tom Hanks fights for his rights in the court of law as he is fired from his organisation on the grounds of having HIV-AIDS due to a gay relation. The actor got the Academy Award and this film put forward the issue of discrimination in the workplace due to HIV-AIDS, homosexuality and homophobia. So a greater coverage related to sexual orientation and sexuality started to gain visibility in different media.

Two prominent films were issued in the year 1997, viz., *Darmiyaan* and *Tamanna* followed by other films. The portrayal of transgenders and homosexuals came up in cinema largely after the year 2000. This representation was largely in a mocking manner. In the year 2003, *Kal Ho Naa Ho* directed by Nikhil Advani got released. This film had situational comedy sequences, where Saif's maid (Kanta Ben) thinks that Shah Rukh Khan and Saif Ali Khan have sexual relations. The very famous Kanta Ben effect came from this film. Later in the film *Maine Pyaar Kyun Kiya*, the actor Sohail Khan wears a towel around his waist and on its back it is written "Not Allowed". So a trend of making sex-oriented jokes with indirect reference to homosexuality started in Bollywood cinema. The films like *Kyaa Kool Hain Hum*, *Dostana*, *Housefull* and *Masti* are some of the films based on this sexual comedy only. But there have been some serious efforts too, like *Honeymoon Travels Private Ltd.*, *Dunno Y Na Jaane Kyun*, *Shabnam Mausi*, *My Brother...Nikhil*, *Fire*, *Welcome to Sajjanpur*, etc. Recently a Pakistani film, *Bol* (*Speak*, 2011) got released all over India. It too has a transgender character and eunuchs.

Even TV is not lagging behind. In a T.V. series *Bigg Boss*, there had been entries of two transgenders in the past, Bobby Darling and Rohit Verma. This time in season five, there is again one transgender Laxmi Narayan, a transgender activist of international repute.[15] All this changes and efforts combined have modified the perspective of the society about "them". Although apprehensions are still there and people mock them "they" co-exist, this has largely been accepted by society.

---

[15] [http://colors.in.com/mena/biggboss, accessed in 2015].

Educative Inserted Messages in Children's Bollywood Cinema.

Karuna Sharma

Indian Film Industry, popularly called Bollywood, constitutes an integral part in the lives of the people of India. Cinema is intertwined in contemporary Indian society and is looked up to for varied gratifications ranging from entertainment to education, this being the least aim. However, the priority regarding the usage of cinema or for that matter any other media has always been different for the government of India. Right from pre-Independence days, attempts have been made to use media for educational purposes. Dadasaheb Phalke, the pioneer of Indian cinema, made educational documentaries such as *The Growth of a Pea Plant* (short, 1911) and *How Films are Made* (short, 1914/15), besides fictional films. Radio experiments in the use of promoting radio for literacy and education were conducted as early as the 1930s. Television was introduced into India by Nehru Government with the primary aim of exploiting the medium for distance education. B.G. Verghese's *Chattera* [in the sixties a column in the *Hindustan Times*, also a model village] experiment attempted to use the daily newspaper to educate Delhiites about rural people and their problems.[1]

Hence, it is quite evident that since time immemorial the various mass communication tools have been used to further social causes. Cinema, hence, has been no exception and attempts have been made to employ this tool to further the education of the people. Education, in this context, is a vast term and encompasses in itself not only the mastery over skills but also the building up of a moral value system, developing scientific temperament and changing the attitude for the acceptance of new ideas. Technology has always been seen as a means

---

[1] Kumar, Keval J. "Mass Communication and Society: Uses, Effects, Representations.", in *Mass Communication in India.* New Delhi: Jaico Publishing House, 2003, p. 332.

to achieve the accomplishment of social objectives in India. However, when films first came to India they were called "actualities" as they were just "visual records of life". Films were introduced in India by the first "cinematographic exhibitions" of the Lumière Brothers, which were held in Bombay on 7 July 1896.[2] The life-like movement created much hype and curiosity amongst people but was not able to retain the audiences for long. As a result this disinterest of the audience led to the artistic potential of this technology.

Another basic reason for the redefinition of the approach concerning this technology constitutes an integral part of human existence. All the major civilisations known to the world have a striking similarity, in that all of these have known to have every expression of art as a vital part of their cultures. Art is the product or process of deliberately arranging items (often with symbolic significance) in a way that influences and affects one or more of the senses, emotions, and intellect. It encompasses a diverse range of human activities, creations, and modes of expression, including music, literature, film, photography, sculpture, and painting.[3]

India, being a place of diverse cultures and traditions, had and still has a consortium of art forms that have played a vital role in the existence of human life in this country. The various uses that any art form is put to are ranging from informing people to entertaining them. As pointed earlier, in a country like India efforts have always been made to utilise art forms as a tool to enhance development initiatives. The concept of development has evolved since World War II from a narrow economistic term into a comprehensive and dynamic one, taking within its ambit almost every aspect of human existence. For, in its fundamental meaning, all development is human development; the focus of development is the human being, the quality of his/her life, and the environment in which that quality is sustained.[4]

Currently, the word development encompasses various aspects; however, the key factor in any development plan, model, strategy or scheme is a change in behaviour concerning its beneficiaries. In this

[2] Kumar, Keval J. "Cinema.", in *Mass Communication in India, op.cit.,* p. 122.
[3] [http://en.wikipedia.org/wiki/Art, accessed 14 October 2011].
[4] Kumar, Keval J. "Mass Media, Culture and Development.", in *Mass Communication in India, op.cit.,* p. 353.

respect, arts and other folk forms have always been a means to bring about this change in behaviour and hence further the goals of development. Films, as an art form and also as a tool of mass communication, have been a means to bring about any desired change by addressing issues of concern. Early films were mythologically oriented and focused primarily on the inculcation of religious beliefs among the people of this country. Successively entertainment and instruction were part of the cinematic representation, in order to make stronger impact on the audiences. The objectives of film making were then made coherent with the social objectives and hence films like *Achhut Kanya* (*The Untouchable Girl*) were made (1936).

The growing awareness regarding the usage of the silver screen for the purpose of extending its influence to a child audience and hence several themes came only in 1955 with the establishment of the Children's Film Society of India (CFSI). Prior to its formation, however, filmmakers made films for the young population of the country. Films for children were made since the 1950s. The first film for children ever produced in India was *Parivartan* (1949) in Bengali, produced by Satyen Bose. This film was remade in Hindi with the title *Jagriti* (S. Bose, *The Awakening*, 1954). Tapan Sinha, a film director, believed that the reason for the inept development of children in India was lack of information and education, and hence supported the making of films that could convey to children issues of social importance in a comprehensible manner. He directed a film called *Kabuliwala* [*The Man from Kabul*] based on Rabindranath Tagore's story in 1950. Another important film for children directed by Prakash Arora, backed by a big banner, was *Boot Polish* (1954) which depicted the lives of two kids belonging to the slums. The film was the story of their struggle to get a dignified life.[5] Despite the making of these films there was no dedicated and religious attempt to promote films for children. There was a need for a separate cinema for children. This inspiration came from Pandit Jawaharlal Nehru, the first Prime Minister of India. Hence on 11 May 1955 the Children's Film Society of India (CFSI) came into being with Pandit Hriday Nath Kunzru as its first President. The CFSI was founded taking into consideration Pandit Nehru's vision of a separate cinema for children.

---

[5] [http://www.cfsindia.org, accessed 14 October 2011].

The anticipated objectives of the CFSI were producing, distributing and exhibiting feature films and short films for children. These films were meant to put forth healthy entertainment that was aimed at enhancing the knowledge and creativity of children, lending them a new vision and helping them shape their life in an independent manner. Also, children are the agents of change in society and whatever change in the communication strategy addressing them is bound to receive better results than any communication directed towards adults. The need and importance of a separate cinema for children has therefore been felt from time to time by many filmmakers. Also, children constitute a major part of the total population of India, which makes it all the more important to have a committed platform which sees to the indulgence of their vibrant energy in a positive manner.

Cinema for Children

India is one of the largest producers of films. The audience of Indian cinema is huge – roughly twelve million a day. To meet this demand, the number of films produced is the largest in the world, currently in the range of eight hundred features a year, more than any other nation. The main centre of production for the popular Hindi cinema is Bombay (now Mumbai), dubbed 'Bollywood' because of its focus on big budget entertainments for the masses.[6] Despite such a humongous production of films, the percentage of films that support a social cause remains negligible. The figures tumble down to a larger extent when it comes to producing films for children. The attention demanded by this group of population is justified if one looks at the huge population of children in India. The total population of children ranging from the age group 0 to 14, according to the census 2001, is 363.61 million approx. The population of children belonging to the age group 5-14 years is 253.1 million approx.[7]

The target audience for the cinema for children is thought to be the second group (from 5-14 years), as per the various studies conducted. It has been found from a research in the West that the pre-operational child (aged 5 years and below), responds differently from the child

---

[6] Wexman, Virginia Wright. "India: A People's Cinema.", in *A History of Film*. New Delhi: Pearson Education, 2007, p. 292.
[7] [http://www.indiastat.com/default.aspx, accessed 14 October 2011].

belonging to the concrete operations stage (6 to 11 years) or to the formal operations stage (11 to 12 years). To illustrate, young children see a series of separate and fragmentary incidents rather than the story of the film. On the contrary, the 6 to 11 years old child understands the story of a film. However, at the age of 10 or 11, he *does* actually understand the feelings and motivations and put himself in the shoes of a character. The 11 to 12 year old group comprehends films as efficiently as adults.

Whatever discussion concerning the plots for these specific films one should not overlook the complex sets of equations that prevail in the Indian context. The country is a mixed bag of overlapping groups which make it difficult to generalise. The country cannot be governed, studied or analysed by a single set of notions and this reflects on its cultural products (films in this case). Due to this variety of cultures, languages, norms and values the social issues also get diversified and large. The magnification of issues due to the conglomeration of multiplicity in India is a phenomenon which has to be understood by a filmmaker. As evident, cinema constitutes also a tool for the improvement of society, and children are considered the most receptive recipients of any communication. Subsequently the cinema for children has always a moral lesson in its narration. Although unnoticed, this genre of cinema gets its due share of attention occasionally, when a filmmaker ventures into the area and portrays issues through the celluloid. The films made for children in India are mostly presented with an approach that is in cognisance with their understanding. These issues are varied ranging from social issues to moral issues; both of them are viewed as specific in building personality in children and hence contributing to the larger picture of development. Many films have been produced by independent film makers as well as the Children's Film Society of India.

Films under Study

This study is based on three films that were targeted for an audience of children - *Makdee* (2002) by Vishal Bhardwaj, *I am Kalam* (2011) by Nila Madhab Panda and *Return of Hanuman* (2007) by Anurag Kashyap. The issues in all the three films are different, but the motive behind them is to inculcate in children the necessity to reconsider a few issues which are now seminal in India and are in perspective essential to its development. All the three films deal with three core issues that demand attention. These are superstition in *Makdee,* literacy in *I am Kalam* and pollution in *Return of Hanuman.* Although the tone remains entertaining, yet there is a strong communication regarding these three prime issues that have kept the government on its heels.

The article 51 A (h) of the Constitution of India states: "It shall be the duty of every citizen of India to develop the scientific temper, humanism and the spirit of inquiry and reform".[8] Superstition in India is seen as a hindrance to the process of growth and development. Superstitions can affect both the very basic elements of life or magnify its reach to broader aspects of living. The first film under discussion is *Makdee* which highlights the extent of superstition prevalent in India. *Makdee* (meaning spider in English), promoted as *The Web of The Witch* in English, is a film for children in Hindi directed by Vishal Bhardwaj, starring Shabana Azmi, Makrand Deshpande, Shweta Prasad, and Alaap Mazgaonkar.[9] The film was released in the year 2002. The plot is set in a village where the legend of a witch living in an old mansion is rife. This witch is supposedly known to change all those who enter the mansion into animals. The place is abandoned and no one enters it. The protagonist in the film, however, is a girl named Chunni, who also has a twin sister named Munni.

The film begins with a scene in which a boy after stealing a hen from a henhouse tries to escape. Being followed by the villagers he enters the forbidden mansion. The film underscores the superstition prevalent among the natives when one of them (who has been the victim of the thefts committed by the boy) beseeches the witch, who apparently lives inside the mansion and who no one has seen, to change the thief into a donkey. The film silently underpins the subservience of the villagers to this belief, or rather the disbelief in the existence of a witch inside that mansion. The film, however, takes Munni into a turbulent journey, one that splits her emotionally between guilt and grief, because she commits the mistake which makes her twin sister

[8] Kashyap, C Subhash. "Fundamental Duties Part IVA, Article 51 A.", in *Our Constitution: An Introduction to India's Constitution and Constitutional Law*. New Delhi: National Book Trust, 2009, p. 162.
[9] [http://en.wikipedia.org/wiki/Makdee, accessed 16 October 2011].

enter the mansion and come out changed into a hen. The film beautifully depicts the dilemma of Munni who is split between playing both Chunni and Munni to hide the disappearance of her sister Chunni. The scene in which Shweta Prasad, who plays the protagonist, thinks that her twin-sister has been turned into a hen holds immense interest. The tumultuous journey, however, also helps her find the truth underneath the mansion and the witch.

The school teacher in the film is a character who continually denies the existence of any evil soul anywhere in this world. A scientific disposition is being promoted through this character, one which helps make a balance between the possible (reality) and the impossible (rumour). The film then gradually brings various moments in which there is a clash between science and superstition. The case in point here is a scene from the film in which the school teacher is underscoring the vitality of being inquisitive and is explaining why someone should try to find out the reasons underneath any phenomenon, happening, belief, rumour. He firmly tells the students that superstition among people has given rise to the concepts of witches, ghosts, etc. He encourages them to find answers and not believe anything blindly. However, this is drastically countered by the presence of the witch outside the classroom in a swing. This witch, however, is visible only to Munni. The film also tries to delve into the various aspects of child psychology. The film is weaved around the grave issue of superstition, a belief that although theorically denied in Indian society remains covertly accepted in reality. Even the people who are considered agents of change and opinion leaders within the society, as the *mukhiya* (the village leader) in *Makdee*, at times do not completely discard these unscientific beliefs. The film tries to throw light upon this conflict between "seeing is believing" and "believing without seeing".

The film is an attempt at inciting a scientific temperament in children, which is a much sought virtue in a developing country like India. The film also subtly underlines how livelihood concerns are primary in a human being's life. The case in point here is the scene towards the end of the story, one featuring Kallu Kasai (Kallu the butcher), a character in the film who is constantly worrying about his henhouse and hence the livelihood that he earns from it. Although Kallu has so far believed in the legend that prevails in the village, yet after losing his hens he supports the view of entering the mansion and finding out the truth. The truth, which earlier for him did not require any testimony, suddenly becomes an equation that has to be substantiated by facts. The character, earlier in the film, had debated about the existence of the witch with the school teacher but now a need to delve into the mystery pops up in his mind. The legend concerning an apparition turns out to be untrue as the mystery gets unravelled. The witch in the mansion turns out to be a lady who had occupied the place in search of an antique idol that is supposedly buried in the mansion's well. The triumph of logical analysis over blind belief is achieved in the end. The film subsequently proves to children that development is inevitable in the absence of superstitions and obscurantism.

Another film under study is Nila Madhab Panda's *I am Kalam* starring Harsh Mayar, Gulshan Grover and Hussan Saad. The film was released in India in the year 2011. The central character in the film is a little Rajasthani boy, Chhottu (played by Harsh Mayar) who wishes to study. Poverty stricken, her mother leaves him to an acquaintance, Bhati (Gulshan Grover), who lives in the city and runs a roadside hotel. While working in the hotel he once sees a news story about Dr. A.P.J Abdul Kalam, the former president of India, and gets impressed. Life takes a new path for Chhottu, who is a bright boy and is keen on learning whatever he can, and starts calling himself Kalam. The film then introduces another kid, Kunwar Rannvijay Singh (Hussan Saad), who is from the royal family of that region and enjoys all the luxuries of life. He is a brilliant boy but craves for a companion, as he is allowed to play with kids belonging to rich families only. However, there are no friends around for him and this saddens him. The film makes a satire on the hypocrisy of the so-called royal blood people who are still basking in the glory of their past and have not moved ahead in the time continuum. They have decided to cling to the past and deny the present in which democracy has allowed fundamental rights to all and sundry.

The film here, quietly but strongly, showcases the "upper class mentality" by underscoring the annoyance of Rannvijjay's father who prevents him from mingling with local kids. Chhottu, who is now Kalam, and Rannvijay somehow get along with each other and become friends. They help each other in everything including studies. Kalam helps Rannvijay with Hindi and in turn learns English from him. The circumstances take an unexpected turn and Kalam is accused of stealing Rannvijay's belongings. Kalam sets off for New Delhi, the capital of

India, to meet the president. Unaware of his departure, the people at the hotel and also Rannvijay's household start searching for him as the misunderstanding regarding the theft gets clarified. The film ends on a positive note as Rannvijay's father realises his mistake and announces he wants to fund Kalam's education. The issues of illiteracy, child labour and caste superiority are strongly weaved in this film, making consequently children aware of all the three issues that are rife in Indian society. Awareness generation leads to a sensibility that ultimately results in making small contributions towards the larger picture. The issue of poverty is also mentioned in the beginning of the film, when the protagonist's mother leaves him with Bhati so to gain some money. Literacy remains the pre-requisite of development and growth, as poverty is an upshot of illiteracy and is followed by another offshoot which is child labour.

The third film under study is *Return of Hanuman* which accentuates the issue of pollution. Pollution is a global issue and hence the film, although deriving its characters from Indian mythology, has a modern tone. *Return of Hanuman* (previously *Hanuman Returns*) is a Hindi animation film about an adventure of the Hindu God Hanuman. It has been stated that the film is not a sequel to *Hanuman* (2005); it has an independent storyline. It is produced by the Percept Picture Company and is directed by Anurag Kashyap. It is a film for children and has been rated as an Educational Film by the Central Board of Film Certification (CBFC), because it deals with the issue of global warming. It was released in India on 28 December 2007.[10]

The film begins with a story being narrated from Indian mythology which describes a great battle between the *Devas* (angels according to Hindu mythology) and the *Asuras* (demons according to Hindu mythology). Hindu mythology states that the *Devas* reside in *Swarglok* (Heaven) and are in charge of rain, harvest, climate, etc. while the *Asuras* live in *Patallok* (Underworld Hell) and oppose the *devas* and want to snatch out their power and hence *Swarglok*. The battle between the angels and the demons ends when Lord Vishnu, the mentor of the world according to Hindu mythology, intervenes in and throws Shukracharya, the mentor of the *asuras* to *Shukra Grah* (planet Venus). An anguished Shukracharya predicts that although all attempts at saving

---

[10] [http://en.wikipedia.org/wiki/Return_of_Hanuman, accessed 16 October 2011].

humanity from the *asuras*, in *Kali Yuga* the humanity will become demon-like. They will be greedy, selfish and will be responsible for their end. *Kali Yuga* (lit. "age of the male demon Kali", or "age of vice") is the last of the four stages that the world goes through as part of the cycle of *yugas* described in Indian scriptures. The other ages are *Satya Yuga*, *Treta Yuga* and *Dvapara Yuga*.[11]

The film changes totally from a mythological set-up to a contemporary one. Lord Hanuman, living in *Swarglok*, sees a small boy being bullied by hooligans and hence decides to incarnate as a human being in order to save the kid. The incarnation of a God is a concept from Hindu mythology which forms the foundation of the rest of incidents. The movie takes a modern backdrop after the birth of Lord Hanuman as Maruti in a Brahmin's (the uppermost caste according to the Hindu caste system) household. The film gradually moves on with Maruti playing pranks, teaching lessons to the hooligans and also to the local goons. However, between all this the prediction made by Shukracharya takes the shape of a monster inside a volcano. The monster is described as the Plastic Monster which has emerged because of the disrespect towards nature by mankind. Brahma, the creator according to the Hindu school of thought, announces his incapability in tackling with the monster. Incapability shown by Gods is an impossible thought in India.

India is a country in which when a big crisis event or calamity takes place people trust Gods rather than their own efforts. The article 'Politicians Pleasing the Rain-Gods: Religious Backwardness in India' by Manoj TV calls attention to the practice adopted by the Madhya Pradesh government of performing *Soma Yagna* [offering of soma juice], a rite in which offerings are made to the deity who according to Hindu scriptures is responsible for bringing rain. This is in sharp contrast to Government's own ruling in Article 51 A. Shockingly, the MP Council of Science and Technology had granted Rs 800,000 for organizing the *yagnas* under a scheme "Scientific authentication of traditional/indigenous knowledge".[12] Hence, a God acknowledging his inability in the film makes the target audience understand the severity of

---

[11] [http://en.wikipedia.org/wiki/Kali_Yuga, accessed 16 October 2011].
[12] [http://nirmukta.com/2009/07/11/politicians-pleasing-the-rain-gods-religious-backwardness-in-india/, accessed 16 October 2011].

the situation. Then, Hanuman shoulders the onus of helping the world get rid of this monster and enters the volcano. The film, however, ends on a positive note as the volcanic eruption that brings out the plastic monster is sent back to the volcano by removing the blockage caused by plastic bottles and other non-biodegradable materials. The blockage is removed by Hanuman *aka* [alias] Maruti who after this goes back to heaven.

In all the three films, the core motive of the filmmakers resides in the contribution to the development of the country by discussing subjects of substance. The first film *Makdee* when dealing with the issue of superstition highlights it as a hindrance in the process of development. Literacy, the issue dealt in *I am Kalam*, is considered a building block of growth and development. However, the issue of pollution, portrayed in *Return of Hanuman*, is a problem that crops up as a consequence of development.

Approach

The approach in all the three films has been a simple one so that the burden of these grave issues of superstition, illiteracy and pollution may be felt by the primary target audience, meaning kids. These hardcore issues, in all the three films, are communicated corresponding to their understanding. The entertainment quotient, in all these films, has been taken care of.

Representation and Stereotyping

In Stuart Hall's book *Representation: Cultural Representations and Signifying Practices*, the practices of representation have been established as one of the key processes of the Cultural Circuit. Representation connects meaning and language to culture. Representation means using language to say something meaningful about, or to represent, the world meaningfully to other people. Representation is an essential part of the process by which meaning is produced and exchanged between the members of a specific culture. It *does* involve the use of signs, of language or images which stand for or represent things. Representation refers to the construction in any medium (especially mass media) of aspects of "reality" such as people, places, objects, events, cultural identities and other abstract concepts. Such representations may be in speech or writing as well as in still or moving pictures.[13]

In the context of this study, representation refers to the depiction of certain individuals and their lifestyles in films produced for children in India. Reality is always represented – what we treat as "direct" experience is "mediated" by perceptual codes. Representation always involves "the construction of reality". The representation in the cinema for children and in the "mainstream" cinema has not changed since the time films have been made in the country. The context of the present has, however, undergone a sea change and hence the reality of our villages, the individuals residing in these villages, their associations, their understanding, their cultural backdrop. This however, is not considered in contemporary films.

Children in all these three films belong to a less privileged background. All their plots are set in villages. Munni the protagonist of *Makdee* belongs to a village in North India, Chhottu or Kalam, the central character of *I am Kalam*, belongs to a village in Rajasthan and then comes to a *dhaba* (roadside hotel) to work and Maruti, the incarnation of Lord Hanuman in *Return of Hanuman*, belongs to a village called Bajarangpur. The representation of a village and hence of the children inhabiting those villages remains identical in all the three pictures. However, the details regarding the accessories, dress, and language have been kept in mind in the two live action films *Makdee* and *I am Kalam*. The third film breaks free from the representational norms of the Indian films in many areas.

The village looks almost similar in both *Makdee* and *I am Kalam* notwithstanding the difference in terrain. Walter Lippman, a social psychologist, in the early 1920's formulated the term "stereotype". He described it as "the picture of the world that a person has in his/her head". As a picture it is definite, which in turn means that it reduces the world to simple characteristics which are represented as permanent by nature. It is the process of attaching attributes to a group of people who follow certain beliefs. It may not be true of all individuals in the group, but stereotyping involves attributing to all those characteristics that are

---

[13] Hall, Stuart (Ed.). *Representation: Cultural Representations and Signifying Practices.* New Delhi: Sage and the Open University, 1997.

present in some members. It reduces and excludes information and exaggerates persons or groups of people to a simplified picture. Chhottu and Laptan of *I am Kalam*, Kallu Kasai, Mugl-e-azam (Chunni's friend) and the thief in the first sequence of *Makdee* are all wearing a black thread around their necks. The black threads are worn (it is believed) to escape from any ill or bad omen. The representation of people inhabiting the village has been such in the Indian cinema. The villagers are regarded as people who are religious to an extent where the line between superstition and believing becomes blurred. The stereotype here lies in the fact that both the movies, although they are set in two different parts of India, have a similar portrayal of the villagers. The notion of villagers being superstitious and ignorant is promoted through this accessory. This representation of people in villages in cinema has remained the same, since long.

Another important conclusion that can be drawn is that all the problems concerning development whenever elucidated in movies take into account the underprivileged backdrop. This holds sense to some extent as poverty and illiteracy are the root causes of many problems in India. However, the shared culture all Indians are a part of is not different in the rural and urban backgrounds. Hence, rural areas are not alone responsible for underdevelopment. Umpteen underprivileged situations (due to poverty and illiteracy) can be found in the urban areas of the country. Hence, the practice of setting up plots in the villages is a stereotype that has been followed in all the three movies under study.

Relating superstition to villages is again a stereotype that is evident in *Makdee*. This reinforces the belief that the inhabitants of villages are bound to be gullible and believe anything without applying any logic. This stealthily confirms the idea that urban backgrounds do not succumb to superstition. This, however, does not hold true in the case of the Indian context. Illiteracy is a problem that is seen in the urban settings of the country too, but the filmmakers always recur to the expedient of the village in depicting this problem. Moreover, household life in a village is portrayed on similar stereotyped lines when it comes to the representation of everyday family habits. Let's consider eating for instance. The film underlines the commonly held belief that food is taken inside the kitchen and that the family members eat together. This is an oversimplified portrayal and can profoundly affect the conclusions we draw about the lifestyle in villages. Furthermore, this might not hold true for all villages, as the country is under a process of rapid urbanisation and the villages are not untouched by this phenomenon. The beliefs held true about villages in primitive India are all melting down to form new definitions.

Return of Hanuman: Breaking the Stereotypes

The third film, as mentioned earlier, is a breakthrough when examining the representational norms and stereotypes followed by Indian film industry. There are many features that have been portrayed in the same fashion for a long time in Indian films. The film takes a new approach and breaks the age-old customs of following a particular kind of depiction. Firstly, the very theme of the film is one which has always had an urban association in the minds of people. The movie talks of pollution which is seen as an urban problem. However, the film shows pollution in a rural set-up. The fact that the rising pollution in the country is not only occurring in the cities is put up in the film. Pollution is an outcome of ignorance on the part of the people living in any part of a country and not of the urban residents alone.

Secondly, the sanctity of the Hindu gods has always been maintained through various ways. The illustration of Gods in Indian Cinema has been a serious one. However, this film shows Gods as techno freaks and the language spoken by them is fairly informal and resembles the everyday tongue in contemporary usage. The language of the Gods, *devas* and even *asuras* in other films dealing with mythology, has been linguistically pure. The tone of the film is rather casual, perhaps because it is an animated movie. The concept of *asuras* has been dealt in different manners in Indian films. However, the creation of a monster as a result of polluting practices stands high as a new way in representing evil. The definition and meaning of *Kala Yuga* is made comprehensive for kids so that they can authenticate it by seeing the same problem existing around them.

Thirdly, the jokes knitted around gods in the beginning are not usual in Indian cinema. This indeed is a fearless attempt in a country like India where anything said, written or shown against the Supreme is blasphemy. The film intelligently uses mythological characters to make a point that is valid in the contemporary world. The film educates in its own informal way.

Although the film maker in this film breaks free of all the commonly used symbols and portrayals, yet he shows his obsequiousness to the superiority of Brahmins. As per the story of the film *Lord Hanuman*, in which the god incarnates as a child in the village Bajarangpur within a Brahmin house. This confirms the fact that the age-old beliefs and values are so ingrained in the people in India that however innovative we want to be the shackles of our complex context tether us to the old.

Conclusion

The contribution of films towards development is an objective that has been maintained with the government since the inception of this art form. The virtues of honesty and punctuality have been promoted before shifting to the promotion of current themes like superstition, literacy, pollution. *Putaani Party*, a Kannada film released in the year 2009 and winner of the National Film Award for Best Children's Film for the year 2009, talks about children's contribution to the local self-government. The issues put forth through Children's Cinema will grow in versatility and with the need of the hour. Children's Cinema needs to be taken up with new vigour so that development initiatives can be communicated and goals reached.

Love, Power and Identity: the Three Faces of Food in Indian Cinema.

Giulia Tedesco

In India live Hindus, Muslims, Sikhs, Buddhists, Jains, Jews and Christians: their daily habits are different, their features are different, even multiple languages and alphabets coexist. In India eighteen official languages and fifty-two dialects are spoken at least; the official language is Hindi, but it is incomprehensible to many people. Therefore, it is not surprising that films are produced in eighteen different languages. It is estimated that even today more than the 80% of national production is in regional languages. Official statistics and Indian critics themselves classify these films on the basis of the language with which they are distributed. The regional films are a very strong instrument of cultural identity, where many different ethnic and religious groups find themselves represented.

The cinema in Tamil has a commercial footprint and it plays in South India the same role that Bollywood plays in the north. Tamil films retain many features belonging to Bollywood: the conventional structure, the star system, the production system. What varies is their content and style. Featuring in the films of Tamil Nadu are the political and nationalist ideologies that call for the release from Brahmin hegemony and from the dominance of the north upon the south. However, even Bollywood has begun to take the same road by focusing more and more on issues of contemporary politics.

There are many similarities between Telugu and Tamil cinemas: an impressive and highly commercial film production and political involvement in films are the most visible. Telugu cinema has developed rapidly since the advent of sound and today it is stated among the first producers of Indian films. The style is in line with Bombay and Madras, but it differs in music and dancing, which derive from local tradition albeit with a few modern reinterpretations. Regarding the theme of Eros, the model is inspired by Hollywood, although in soft version because of the strict rules of censorship.

We can just talk about Malayalam films since 1951. Unlike other states, Malayalam films were not inspired by mythology, but by literature. However, excluding the choice of subjects and some care in representing all the religious communities of the area, the stylistic characteristics of the Malayalam films are similar to the productions of the other regions.

Kannada cinema has had a late start due to the obtrusive presence of Madras, which has dominated South Indian film production for several years. The real development of the Kannada film occurs in the late '60s, when production increased from 35 to 60 films a year. From the '70s onwards it bloomed in parallel commercial cinema and art cinema. The latter typology is firmly established in 1970 with the film *Samskara.*

If one moves from the state of Karnataka to Bihar, one hears a different language: Bhojpuri. Bhojpuri film history begins in 1962 with the well-received film *Ganga Maiyya Tohe Piyari Chadhaibo* (roughly, *O Mother Ganga I'll Offer You the Yellow Cloth*, 1962). Bhojpuri cinema can be divided into three phases: the first period (1962-68) started with the film *Ganga Maiyya Tohe Piyari Chadhaibo*, the second period (1969-1976) during which only one film was produced, and the last period in which Bhojpuri cinema bursts back to life with the movie *Dangal* (*The Bout*, 1977). Then, in the five years between 2004 and 2008, over 275 Bhojpuri films have been produced. "The fledgling cottage industry of the 1960s has now become a blusting regional film industry [...]. Now big-budget films are shot in Cinema Scope and some have even shot abroad [...]".[1] Thematically, the majority of Bhojpuri films are family dramas but there are also mythological films. In recent years, the genre has attracted Bollywood biggies. Finally, it is worth remembering that Bhojpuri cinema became the target of sectarian violence aimed at migrants from Uttar Pradesh in 2007: once again, a

---

[1] Ghosh, Avijit. *Cinema Bhojpuri*. London: Penguin Book, 2010, pp. 2-3.

piece of living history was told through the camera. Now, Bhojpuri films are reviewed almost on a par with Bollywood films.

Since the birth of Indian cinema in 1913, Bollywood films have taken a special place in Indian popular culture and are still deeply affecting it. Usually built on a system of six songs and at least two lavish ballets, each of these films is usually focused on seven major themes: an impossible love that knows no borders, the conflicts between children and parents, a great revenge, redemption, the fight for survival in adverse conditions, the maintenance of honour and dignity and a strong and nearly universal respect for religious and moral values. The recurring motifs that characterise Bollywood movies (with a standard running time of 180 minutes) are an integral part of the intrigue, whose ending is usually more than predictable.

What draws the audience to them is the familiarity of the stories mixed with the appearance of glamorous and famous actors (so beautiful and unreachable to be assimilated to gods), with melodious and rhythmic music (often, real disco dance), with exotic landscapes or very posh and rich entourage (sometimes, so much to seem unreal, fairy-tale scenarios). Some plots are taken from Hollywood industry, but they are so adapted to the Indian canon of representation to be almost unrecognisable. Having said that, of course, the happy ending is assured. Since the '90s, there is no newspaper or magazine that does not devote a space to current Bollywood. Everyone loves the movies of Bollywood, everyone follows Bollywood: attitudes, values and people who can afford it even in material objects such as clothing or styles of interior design. What Bollywood likes, the vast majority of Indian population likes.

Bengali cinema has features of its own. The presence of the British in Bengal has made necessary the creation of a middle class educated according to a Western parameter. This social class, the *bhadralok*, has promoted a hybrid Indian-Western culture and has given birth to a movement of national liberation. The Bengali intellectual elite saw the cinema as a resource for creative art and as a means to advance their ideas and their ideologies. The Film Society was established precisely to promote the study of cinema and its techniques. Since the '70s onwards, thanks to the funding policy of the Government of Bengal, a new generation of filmmakers has been created, these renowned also in Europe (e.g. the director Aparna Sen with her first film *36 Chowringhee Lane* (1981). We cannot but mention here one of the representatives of the "new cinema" in India, Gautam Ghose, whose political and social commitment oozes from many of his films.

As a matter of fact, such a great multitude of regional realities has also a huge amount of spectators, who, of course, have one thing in common: the feeling of being represented and, at the same time, the desire to emulate what is transmitted from the film. Because every stage performance, and therefore every movie, sends messages. A film sends many messages, through various types of codes, such as, for example, the nutritional one: the nutritional ritual is a very special moment in a script, a moment that everyone in the audience lives every day; it also becomes a key moment of each film, thanks to the multiplicity of meanings it can hold.

"Filmi food" has a particular feature: it is an observed food, filmed and constructed specifically to be seen through the camera, to be proposed to the audience. Of course, the mode of consumption of this meal will be virtual, visual, but no less important. Indeed, analysing what is served, how and by whom food is eaten on the scene, one can find details of the messages sent to the public right through the meal itself. "In [...] films [...] food could be [...] used to enhance a scene, help delineate the story, define character, suggest motivation, reveal states of mind, indicate social class or satirize a cultural tradition".[2]

Both food and the nutritional rituals embody knowledge, codes, customs and preferences coming from every culture and at the same time they reveal them. The message transmitted to the public through the feature of the meal is very strong and almost unconsciously taken in immediately. Among other things, many taboos are inherent in the consumption of food. These taboos are in a sense similar to those that revolve around the world of Eros. Food and love then. It is not the first time that these two elements have been associated. Food not consumed can represent a not consumed passion, thus becoming an object of desire itself in a meal that can never be eaten together by the protagonists of the film *Bandini* (1963). Food, however, may also have

---

[2] Zimmerman, Steve, and Ken Weiss. *Food in the Movies*. London: McFarland & Co., 2005, p. 161.

political significance: whoever controls it has the power and as it
happens in the film *Roti Kapada aur Makaan* (*Food, Clothing and
Shelter*, 1974) may control the labour market, too. Food and its lack can
also lead to violence.

Still, we must not forget how the culinary traditions of a country
are a sign of ethnic distinction in which many migrants find their
identity. Indians abroad search in Indian food their own India. Films set
outside the boundaries of India have significance because they represent
the mode of adaptation of Indians abroad, their difficulties, their
achievements or their oscillations in identity: the food shown in these
films talks about the culture it comes from and about the mixed feelings
of people who consume it. What we are is what we eat: cooking Indian
food abroad underlines a choice of belonging that the protagonists of
The Namesake (2006) make between being Americans and continuing
to be Indians. In the movies much attention is paid to the cinematic
representation of food. That happens for example in the film *The
Namesake*, in which a pan full of cooking *samosas* is filmed. Then we
proceed to the analysis of four Indian films about the relationship
between love and food, food and power and food as identity.

Cheeni Kum (2007). That Little Bit Extra.

Cheeni Kum [*Less Sugar*] is a film that warrants, although designed
to be enjoyed particularly by a Western taste, the ingredients of the
typical *masala* movie. Although there are seven songs, they are not
combined with choreography, but rather contribute the soundtrack of
the film. Even the plot, concentrating on the large difference in age
between the two protagonists, is quite unusual for Bollywood. Yet, as in
any good Indian movie, the happy ending is assured after many
vicissitudes and troubles.

Food is the real protagonist of the film: a touch of extra sugar that
serves to soften the heart of Buddhadev Gupta (Amitabh Bachchan),
owner of the finest Indian restaurant in London and head chef. A pinch
of sugar that comes from the sweetness and strength of the female
protagonist, thirty years junior, Nina Verma (Tabu). The first meeting
between the two is quite troublesome and happens inside Buddhadev's
restaurant, when Nina sends back an inedible (because too sweet)

Hyderabadi Zafarani Pulao. Buddhadev does not admit of such a thing in its own restaurant: "cooking" he says "is the finest art in the world: eyes, nose, tongue are involved" and no one can accuse him of having prepared a dish, a work of art, good only for a "fraud Indian restaurant". Therefore, the two characters meet because of food: she rejects something that he cooked and then, indirectly, himself. A different reaction is staged when Buddhadev eats with his mother. Notwithstanding the possibility of having food in his restaurant, Buddhadev eats every day at home. He complains about her homemade food but appreciates it for the sense of domesticity and warmth that it conveys. It should be observed that Buddhadev always eats alone. In fact, like a good traditional Indian woman, his mother eats by herself in the kitchen and not with her husband and children. This habit originates from the sense of pure and impure around which turn the class, caste and sex divisions of Indian world. A woman, being inferior to a man in rank, could contaminate her husband (or son) by sharing with him the same food. But this concerns the ancient traditions, followed by the old mother of the protagonist. In the next scene these same traditions are not respected: the two protagonists are chatting over a coffee in Buddhadev's restaurant. All employees now have sensed that Buddhadev is in love with Nina and so they nickname her "*Zafarana Pulao*". The female protagonist is actually identified with a dish! But there is more: at their first official date, Buddhadev calls Nina "*Leg Kebab*", because of Nina's passion for chicken. In the middle of the story, Buddhadev cooks a new dish of his own invention based on chicken only for his beloved Nina.

The culinary weapon will be used to conquer the favour of Nina's father, Omprakash Verma, unfortunately with little success. Buddhadev prepares a vegetarian meal that does not meet the tastes of Omprakash, who loves chicken meat more than any other dish. Here food unites daughter and father: for both of them chicken is their favorite dish. But once Nina's father knows the intention of the two lovers to marry he starts a fast, so as to starve himself, since he is totally against their marriage because of the difference in age between the two. The jealousy that consumes Omprakash, consumes him just like thirst and hunger. However, Omprakash surrenders in the end and the last scene is a shot around a meal cooked by Buddhadev, for his wife and his in-law. Buddhadev's mother mocks Nina's father: "You are lucky. One is lucky to be served food by one's daughter. But you are making your son-in-law serve food for you". Traditionally, it should be the daughter-in-law to serve food, not her husband.

Roti Kapada aur Makaan (1974). The Three Basic Needs.

To save his family from poverty, Bharat (Manoj Kumar) joins a gang of entrepreneurs devoted to illegal traffics: they hide food and other commodities to make prices rise and to bring down the government of India under protests at the same time. But eventually, Bharat decides to redeem himself and with his brother, a soldier by profession, unmasks the traitors to the nation. In this way prices and wages will again be balanced. Meanwhile, Bharat also rescues a woman from selling herself (in exchange for some drugs). Finally they get married.

Food in this film is the need that pushes people to do anything. Who owns it has the power. Who has not suffers violence and hunger. So, in this case food is presented as the fulcrum of society and of its social rules. Rules that are freely broken by those who, in the general poverty, have access to food. The girl whom Bharat marries at the end of the story tells how she has been raped, by the owner of a shop with two henchmen of the local mafia. In the scene showing the girl's flash back, the rape is filmed in the go-down adjacent to the store, in which all the stolen flour has been hidden. In this scene, the girl asks for some flour and in return she is raped on the heap of flour. The connection is immediate: to have some food she must sell her body. There is no justice. Those who have food, they disregard the laws. In the middle of the film, there is even a song dedicated to inflation: "Holding money in hand we used to bring sugar in a bag, now money come in the bag and sugar in the hand". Then it continues: "The adulteration of sugar killed us, the cream of the milk power killed us". It is the food itself the weapon pointed against those who have lost their jobs because of inflation. Inflation is caused by food shortage. No food, no jobs. No work, no clothes (*kapadia*) or home (*makaan*) or bread (*roti*). A noose tightens more and more, *ad infinitum*.

The Namesake (2006). Identity in Food.

The Namesake tells the story of a family and its difficulties in adapting to a foreign country. The family is composed of Ashoke (father), Ashima (mother), Gogol (son) and a daughter; the son as an adult is the male protagonist of the second part of the story. The food shot in this film embodies the dilemmas of identity of the protagonists.

The first "gastronomic scene" takes place in the kitchen of the family house in New York, where Ashima has just moved with Ashoke. Ashima is stunned by the new climate and by the city. She is cold and she is waiting for her husband back home to have some companionship. When Ashoke comes back from work Ashima wants to brew him a cup of tea. But seeing her in bad shape, Ashoke tells her to go to bed, where he will serve her evening bed tea: "as we use here," Ashoke says to his wife who looks at him dumbfounded. A few minutes later Ashoke leaves home. Then Ashima jumps out of bed and runs towards the cupboard and almost obsessively tries to find some rice and some spices, but she finds only Rice Krispies, some red chili powder extra hot and peanuts. However she mixes all together and eats feverishly with a spoon. As a matter of fact Ashima tries to feel again at home in the unfamiliar and cold greyness of New York. To achieve that she would turn to well-known domestic flavours, but she is obliged instead to wolf down an unlikely *masala*.

Later in the film, Ashima offers a *lassi* (a traditional Indian yogurt-based drink) to Gogol's American girlfriend. It's obvious that Ashima does not approve of this girl. Afterwards, the scene is shifted at lunch, Ashima has cooked Indian food: "Your mother has been in the kitchen for two days to prepare this meal," says Ashoke to his son and indirectly to the American girl. The parents eat with their right hands, whereas the two young people use cutlery. The difference between the second generation migrant, Gogol and his parents Ashoke and Ashima is enormous. Old people are trying to remain firmly anchored to their traditions, their only certainties in that extraneous world (despite all the time they have spent in America), whereas Gogol stands in-between the Indian and Western worlds. So he is the only link (although a very fragile one) between his Indian parents and the young American girl sitting *among* not *with* them.

In the second half of the film Gogol has grown. He has left the
American girl and now he is flirting with a cool Bengali girl who (like
him) feels herself comfortable in the role of an emancipated urbanite in
New York. "My mother is horrified to learn that I'll do not cook Indian
food for you" she says to him, while two pans full of oil and meat are
sizzling on the stove in the modern kitchen. Conversely, it should be
noted that later in the story she fries some *samosas* with her mother-in-
law. Obviously she is now married to Gogol. At that moment she
receives a phone call ... her mistress? It is clear the association in this
scene between Indian traditional food, here represented by *samosas*, and
the feeling of inner closure which seems to circumscribe the young
wife. Now she is a good Indian wife, no longer a young girl free to be
something different. In those small *samosas* one can indeed rehearse a
contrast between the roles assigned to women in the Indian culture and
those proposed instead by America.

Pyar Ki Kahani (1971). Foodsickness... A Nostalgic Stomach.

Speaking about identities concealed in food now the focus is
shifted on regionalism. Ram Chand (Amitabh Bachchan) becomes a
close friend of Ravi Chand (Anil Dhawan), and when Ravi marries, he
and his wife become like a brother and a sister to Ram. In contrast
however, at the time of Ram's engagement with the young Kusum
Sharma (Tanuja), Ravi does not seem to share his friend's happiness.

Ram works as a peon in a pharmaceutical industry away from his
home region, Punjab. The attachment to his land is very strong in Ram,
so incessantly having dreams of eating *paratha* instead of the *idli* that
he is forced to eat in the canteen of the company. One morning, Kusum
hears Ram that turning over in his sleep speaks about cauliflower
paratha. Ram's nostalgia for the food of his homeland is so strong that
Ravi makes his wife to dress in Punjabi garb and makes her to serve a
Punjabi *thali* for lunch. Ram is so happy that he is on the verge of tears.
So, native food stands here for regional nostalgic belonging. Here
Punjabi food embodies unbroken attachment to one's cultural traditions:
a true Punjabi can only eat *paratha*, whereas a South Indian is crazy for
idli.

Reference

Filmography

Bandini, Bimal Roy, 1963.

Pyar Ki Kahani, Ravee Nagaich, 1971.[3]

Roti Kapada aur Makaan, Manoj Kumar, 1974.

The Namesake, Mira Nair, 2006.

Cheeni Kum, R. Balki, 2007.

Texts

Aime, Elena. *Storia del cinema indiano*. Torino: Lindau, 2007.

Dumont, Louis. *Homo Hierarchicus*: *il sistema delle caste e le sue implicazioni*. Milano: Adelphi, 1991 (1966).

Ghosh, Avijit. *Cinema Bhojpuri*. London: Penguin Books, 2010.

Monti, Alessandro, Irma Piovano, Aelfric Bianchi. *Chalta hai: così va il mondo. Bollywood specchio dell'India*. Alessandria: Edizioni dell'Orso, 2010.

Morsiani, Alberto. *Il cinema indiano*. Roma: Carocci editore, 2009.

Thoraval, Yves. *Les cinémas de l'Inde*. Paris: L'Harmattan, 1998.

Zimmerman, Steve, and Ken Weiss. *Food in the Movies*. London: McFarland & Co., 2005.

---

[3] *Pyar Ki Kahani*, that is, *Story of a Love*.

Filmography

The following list mentions all the films cited in the book. Films appear in chronological order.

The Growth of a Pea Plant (short), Dadasaheb Phalke, 1911.

How Films are Made (short), Dadasaheb Phalke, 1914/15.

Achhut Kanya (*The Untouchable Girl*), Franz Osten, 1936.

Parivartan, Satyen Bose, 1949.

Kabuliwala (*The Man from Kabul*), Tapan Sinha, 1950.

Amar, Mehboob Khan, 1954.

Boot Polish, Prakash Arora, 1954.

Jagriti (*The Awakening*), Satyen Bose, 1954.

Mother India, Mehboob Khan, 1957.

Sujata, Bimal Roy, 1959.

Mughal-e-Azam (*Mughal King*), Karimuddin Asif, 1960.

Ganga Maiyya Tohe Piyari Chadhaibo (*O Mother Ganga I'll Offer You the Yellow Cloth*), Kundan Kumar, 1962.

Bandini, Bimal Roy, 1963.

Dil Ek Mandir (*The Heart, a Temple*), C.V. Shridhar, 1963.

Sangam (*Confluence*), Raj Kapoor, 1964.

Raat Aur Din (*Darkness and Light*), Satyen Bose, 1967.

Samskara, Pattabhirama Reddy, 1970.

Pyar Ki Kahani (*Story of a Love*), Ravee Nagaich, 1971.

Ankur (*The Seedling*), Shyam Benegal, 1973.

Kunwara Baap (*Unmarried Father*), Mehmood Ali, 1974.

Roti Kapada aur Makaan (*Food, Clothing and Shelter*), Manoj Kumar, 1974.

Sholay (*Embers*), Ramesh Sippy, 1975.

Amar Akbar Anthony, Manmohan Desai, 1977.

Dangal (*The Bout*), Rati Kumar, 1977.

Nishant (*When Night Comes*), Shyam Benegal, 1978.

Lawaris (*Bastard*), Prakash Mehra, 1981.

36 Chowringhee Lane, Aparna Sen, 1981.

Maine Pyar Kiya (*My Love Kiya*), Sooraj R. Barjatya, 1989.

Sadak (*Road*), Mahesh Bhatt, 1991.

Chamatkar (*Miracle*), Rajiv Mehra, 1992.

Roja, Mani Ratnam, 1992.

Philadelphia, Jonathan Demme, 1993.

Bombay, Mani Ratnam, 1995.

Daayra (*The Square Circle*), Amol Palekar, 1996.

Fire, Deepa Metha, 1996.

Darmiyaan (*In-Between*), Kalpana Lajmi, 1997.

Tamanna (*Wish*), Mahesh Bhatt, 1997.

Dil Se.. (*The Ways of the Heart*), Mani Ratnam, 1998.

Ghulam (*Slave*), Vikram Bhatt, 1998.

Jeans, Shanmugam Shankar, 1998.

Pyaar Kiya To Darna Kya (*When in Love, No Need to Worry*), Sohail Khan, 1998.

Sangharsh (*Struggle*), Tanuja Chandra, 1999.

Mission Kashmir, Vidhu Vinod Chopra, 2000.

Lagaan (*Tax on Land*), Ashutosh Gowariker, 2001.

Nayak: *The Real Hero*, S. Shankar, 2001.

Maine Dil Tujhko Diya (*I Have Given My Heart To You*), Sohail Khan, 2002.

Makdee (*Spider* promoted as *The Web of The Witch*), Vishal Bhardwaj, 2002.

Mr. and Mrs. Iyer, Aparna Sen, 2002.

Kal Ho Naa Ho (*Whether Tomorrow Comes or Not*), Nikhil Advani, 2003.

Matrubhoomi: *A Nation without Women*, Manish Jha, 2003.

Ab Tak Chhappan (*Till Now Fifty-six*), Shimit Amin, 2004.

Girlfriend, Karan Razdan, 2004.

Masti (*Mischief*: *Oath on Beloved*), Indra Kumar, 2004.

Swadesh, *We the People*, Ashutosh Gowariker, 2004.

Hanuman (animation film), V.G. Samant, Milind Ukey, 2005.

Karam (*Deeds*), Sanjay K. Gupta, 2005.

Kyaa Kool Hain Hum (*How Cool We Are*), Sangeeth Sivan, 2005.

Maine Pyaar Kyun Kiya (*Why I Have Fallen in Love*), David Dhawan, 2005.

My Brother...Nikhil, Onir, 2005.

Page 3, Madhur Bhandarkar, 2005.

Shabnam Mausi (*Aunt Shabnam*), Yogesh Bharadwaj, 2005.

Water, Deepa Metha, 2005.

Bigg Boss (TV Series, 2006-2015).

Rang De Basanti (*Colour of Sacrifice*), Rakeysh Omprakash Mehra, 2006.

The Namesake, Mira Nair, 2006.

Chak De! India, (*Go! India*), Shimit Amin, 2007.

Cheeni Kum (*Less Sugar*), R. Balki, 2007.

Ek Chalis Ki Last Local (*The Last Local of One Forty*), Sanjay Khanduri, 2007.

Honeymoon Travels Private Ltd., Reema Kagti, 2007.

Parzania. Heaven and Hell on Earth, Rahul Dholakia, 2007.

Return of Hanuman (animation film), Anurag Kashyap, 2007.

Dostana (*Friendship*), Tarun Mansukhani, 2008.

Fashion, Madhur Bhandarkar, 2008.

Jodhaa Akbar, Ashutosh Gowariker, 2008.

Rab Ne Bana Di Jodi (*A Couple Made in Heaven*), Aditya Chopra, 2008.

Welcome to Sajjanpur, Shyam Benegal, 2008.

Firaaq (*Separation*), Nandita Das, 2009.

Putaani Party, Ramchandra P. N., 2009.

Dunno Y Na Jaane Kyun (*Don't Know Why*), Sanjay Sharma, 2010.

Housefull, Sajid Khan, 2010.

Lamhaa (*Moment*), Rahul Dholakia, 2010.

Bol (*Speak*), Shoaib Mansoor, 2011.

I am Kalam, Nila Madhab Panda, 2011.

Afterword

The articles collected here are not meant to deal with cinematic analysis. They rather purpose to throw some light on Indian contemporary society and its more relevant aspects, its multicultural identity, the necessity for instruction, or the use of stereotypes. So we can hear the voice of young India, through the contributions of the research scholars, with their involvement in their country and their fresh sense of responsibility.

Other articles give expression to the uneasy feelings concerning the ugly growth of communalism and female foeticide, a reactive frame of mind that is equally found in the articles dealing with the discrimination of the sexual "Other" and the splitting of national identity in Kashmir.

Finally the focus is on domesticity in contemporary marriage, in transition between tradition and modernity, and the ritual of food in everyday life, both at home and abroad, is set against famishing power and the loneliness of the migrant.

For a first approach to the themes (and more equally relevant) this volume deals with, its editors suggest *Les Indiens, voix multiples*, Arundhati Virmani, Boulogne-Billancourt: HD ateliers henry dougier, 2016.

Alessandro Monti

Contributors

Sisir Basu is Professor (former Head) in the Department of Journalism and Mass Communication, Banaras Hindu University, Varanasi, India. MA in Communication (Journalism), University of Philippines, Quezon City, Manila. MS – Television, Radio and Film, Syracuse University, New York, USA. Ph.D. in Communication, University of Philippines, Quezon City, Manila.

Alessandro Monti is Retired Full Professor of English and Contemporary Indian Studies, University of Palermo then University of Torino, Italy. Formerly Head (for six years) of the Department of Oriental Studies (Turin). Member of the National Committee for the evaluation of University Research. Visiting Professor with the Kakatya University (Warangal). Joined the Committee for Commonwealth Studies (Delhi) replacing Mulk Raj Anand after his demise. ICCR Fellow with the Banaras Hindu University. Associated with the Research Centre CESMEO for Advanced Studies in Oriental Studies, Turin and with Le GRIMH in Lyon. Chief Guest in Tirupathi at an International Conference on Indian Contemporary Literature. Speaker in analogous conferences in Edinburgh, Delhi, Trivandrum, Singapore, also speaker in international conferences on Indian and Sanskrit Culture (Milan, Rome, Turin). He founded and directed for 6 years the research international series *DOST* on Oriental Studies with the Department of Oriental Studies, Torino, editing or taking charge of more than 20 books. Previously, he edited the series *Paradoxa* with L'Harmattan, Italy. He published in India with Atlantic Press, Prestige, Women Unlimited and others. Internationally with Greenwood, Hong Kong University Press, University Press of America, Rodopi, Le GRIMH Editions. On the editorial board of *The Journal of Aesthetics* (no more published, Kerala) and on the advisory editorial board of *The Atlantic*

Review of Feminist Studies and of *The Atlantic Critical Review* (International Journals published by Atlantic Publishers).

Neha Pandey is Research Scholar in the Department of Journalism and Mass Communication, Banaras Hindu University, Varanasi, India. MA in Mass Communication, Department of Journalism and Mass Communication, Banaras Hindu University, Varanasi, India. PG Diploma in Journalism, Asian College of Journalism, Chennai. BA in English Literature, Mahila Mahavidyalaya, Banaras Hindu University, Varanasi, India.

Carole Rozzonelli is Associate Professor of English, ICT, and Communications Law (Law of the New Information Technologies, Media and Communications Law) at the Institute of Communication, University Lyon 2, France. Former Deputy Vice-Chancellor in Communications of the University (2008-2012). Associated with the Research Centre PASSAGES XX-XXI and Le GRIMH in Lyon. After specializing in the area of English language and ICT literacy, English literature and cinema, now, she specializes in Media Law, covering both traditional mass media as well as the law of the New Information Technologies. She currently lectures on English, ICT and Media Law. Speaker in conferences in France and also in international conferences on English and ICT (Bergamo, Torino, Antwerp...). She collaborates with Professor Alessandro Monti and has participated in the research international series *DOST* on Oriental Studies with the Department of Oriental Studies, Torino, Italy. Also, she edited the series *DOST Educational*. She published in Italy, India and France with Loescher Editore, L'Harmattan Italia, Edizioni dell'Orso, Atlantic Publishers, CercleS Editions, EADTU, and Le GRIMH Editions. On the advisory editorial board of *The Atlantic Review of Feminist Studies* and of *The Atlantic Critical Review* (International Journals published by Atlantic Publishers).

Karuna Sharma is Research Scholar in the Department of Journalism and Mass Communication, Banaras Hindu University, Varanasi, India. M.Phil. in Mass Communication, Bundelkhand University, Jhansi, Uttar Pradesh. MA in Mass Communication, Apeejay Institute of Journalism and Mass Communication, Dwarka, New Delhi, B.Sc. MBGPG College, Haldwani Kumaon University, Nainital, Uttarakhand.

Shweta is Research Scholar in the Department of Journalism and Mass Communication, Banaras Hindu University, Varanasi, India. MA in Mass Communication, Department of Journalism and Mass Communication, Banaras Hindu University, Varanasi, India. BA in English Literature, Mahila Mahavidyalaya, Banaras Hindu University, Varanasi, India.

Giulia Tedesco is Assistant librarian and proofreader of articles concerning Indian culture. She has graduated in 2011 in *Anthropology and Ethnology* at the University of Turin, specializing in Sociology, Anthropology, Psychology, History, with a thesis on "Fast India: Compromises of Culinary Globalisation". She has also completed a Degree in Intercultural Communication in 2008, her main subjects of study being Hindi and Sanskrit Literature. She has been, from June 2008 to May 2010, employed at CESMEO, International Institute of Advanced Oriental Studies (Turin) and co-worker of Professor Alessandro Monti, Director of the Department of Oriental Studies, University of Turin, collaborating in the writing of the Indian-English reference book *Business India*, (Edizioni dell'Orso, 2010).

Sudarshan Yadav is Research Scholar in the Department of Journalism and Mass Communication, Banaras Hindu University, Varanasi, India. MA in Mass Communication, Department of Journalism and Mass Communication, Banaras Hindu University, Varanasi, India. B.Sc. (2003-2006), Veer Bahadur Singh Purvanchal University, Jaunpur, Uttar Pradesh, India.